SILENT KILLERS

SILENT KILLERS

RADON AND OTHER HAZARDS

BY KATHLYN GAY

Franklin Watts
New York London Toronto Sydney
1988
An Impact Book

Maps and illustrations by Vantage Art

Photographs courtesy of: Gamma/Liaison: pp. 18 (Richard Nichols),
44 (John Chiasson), 75 (Fred Vuich), 76, 102, 104 (Pablo
Bartholomew); UPI/Bettmann Newsphotos: pp. 21, 33, 93;
Sygma: pp. 54 (Tannenbaum), 66 (J.P. Laffont); Photo
Researchers, Inc.: pp. 84 (Joe Munroe), 96 (Georg Gerster).

Library of Congress Cataloging-in-Publication Data
Gay, Kathlyn.
Silent killers: radon and other hazards / by Kathlyn Gay.
p. cm.—(An Impact book)
Bibliography: p.
Includes index.
Summary: Examines potentially dangerous chemicals, gases, and
metals that can unknowingly endanger people in their homes, schools,
and workplaces and destroy the environment.
ISBN 0-531-10598-9
1. Environmental health.   2. Toxicology.   3. Radon—Toxicology.
4. Consumer education.   [1. Environmental health.   2. Toxicology.
3. Consumer education.]   I. Title.
RA566.G36   1988   88-5549
363.1'7—dc19   CIP AC

For Betty,
who personally experiences
the health threat of toxic
materials in the environment
and has provided excellent
research help for this book.

CONTENTS

SILENT KILLERS

1
THE "CHEMICAL SOUP"

Asbestos
Benzene
Carbon Monoxide
Dioxin
Ethylene Dibromide
Formaldehyde
Lead
Mercury
Radon Gas
Styrene
Trichloroethylene

This is only a partial list of potentially dangerous chemicals, gases, and metals that can endanger people in their homes, schools, or workplaces. Over the past few decades, hundreds of natural and manufactured substances found inside buildings and outdoors have been identified as hazards to health and life itself.

Fact: Asbestos, a mineral fiber in insulation and other building materials, is the most widespread toxic substance in the nation, according to a 1987 report by *Consumers' Research* magazine. Between eight thousand and ten thou-

11

sand deaths each year are the result of asbestos-related illnesses such as lung and stomach cancers.

Fact: Groundwater—the source of drinking water for nearly 50 percent of all Americans—has become increasingly contaminated. Such toxic chemicals as benzene, carbon tetrachloride, and trichloroethylene (TCE), which are known as *carcinogens,* or cancer-causing substances, have been found in drinking water supplies in communities across the nation.

Fact: Methylene chloride is a common ingredient in household products such as paint strippers, insecticides, and hair spray and is used to decaffeinate some brands of coffee. Methylene chloride is known to cause cancerous tumors in animals and is widely suspected as a carcinogen in humans.

Fact: Radon gas causes an estimated twenty thousand to thirty thousand lung cancer deaths each year. Radon may be a serious hazard in one out of five of the nation's homes built in areas where granite and other rocks and soils contain uranium that decays and thus produces the radon gas.

Fact: As is well known, lead, if ingested, can cause mental retardation, stunt growth, and even kill. A heavy metal, lead is outlawed as a paint ingredient and is being phased out in gasoline, but the Environmental Protection Agency (EPA) has found high levels of lead, which is leached from the drinking-water pipelines, in many American communities.

Environmental concerns, such as the examples just described, are not new. During the 1960s and 1970s, large numbers of groups and individuals spoke out against the pollution of air, waterways, and land. As a result, the federal government set up the EPA, whose mission is spelled out in its title. The EPA also has the responsibility of enforcing federal environmental laws.

The Clean Air Act of 1963, for example, was the first law that allowed the federal government to take some actions to control air pollution from so-called smokestack industries, such as steel plants and foundries, that spewed heavy smoke and coal fumes into the atmosphere. In 1967, the law was strengthened and was eventually replaced by a Clean Air Act of 1970, which set a specific timetable for curbing smokestack emissions.

Since the 1960s, the quality of surface waters across the United States also has improved. Federal laws restrict the discharge and dumping of wastes into rivers, streams, lakes, and oceans. But at times surface waters have become contaminated with city sewage, biological wastes from medical facilities, and toxic wastes from industries.

In the spring of 1987, for example, untreated sewage from the Sanitary Treatment Plant in Michigan City, Indiana, flowed into a river called Trail Creek. During heavy rains, plant operators had to bypass the overloaded treatment area that purifies wastewater and dump untreated sewage into the river. The result was massive fish kills. A $30 million expansion of the sanitary plant is under way so that bypassing will no longer be necessary in Michigan City.

Heavy rains often put a burden on older sewer systems across the country, forcing water with a high level of fecal coliform, a harmful bacteria, into rivers and lakes. Contaminated waterways threaten not only fish and other wildlife but the health of swimmers as well. Waterborne fecal coliform may cause diarrhea, nausea, and other gastrointestinal problems.

Another federal protective measure, the Safe Drinking Water Act of 1974, bans the use of drinking water that has bacterial and chemical levels above the safety limits set by the law. The U.S. Congress also passed still another protective law, the Toxic Substances Act of 1976, which sets controls on disposal of poisonous wastes, including nuclear waste.

The laws, however, have forced some manufacturing companies to spend huge sums of money to install pollution-control systems, which led to increases in the price of manufactured goods. In other instances, manufacturers closed

13

down because they were unable to pay the costs of the pollution controls. Plant closings meant job losses, particularly in the "rust belt," or midwestern areas where many heavy industries are located.

When President Ronald Reagan took office, many in his administration wanted to "deregulate." They believed strongly that federal regulations hampered economic growth. Thus, from 1980 through 1983, some federal laws to protect and clean the environment were not strictly enforced, and some EPA officials, including the director appointed by Reagan, failed to carry out their duties as environmental protectors, allowing industries to continue to pollute or to stall in cleanup of toxic emissions or wastes. As a result, several EPA officials were forced to resign from their offices as the public called for stronger federal controls on polluters.

At the same time, however, the public continued to demand a variety of convenience goods that can have toxic effects. Styrofoam packaging materials and cleaning compounds are just two examples of products that can pose health hazards but are being manufactured to meet consumer demand.

In some cases, consumers may be unaware of dangers posed by using certain products. Buyers frequently assume that the products in the marketplace are safe, and indeed many federal, state, and local regulations are designed to protect public health and safety. On the other hand, consumers may continue to buy and use hazardous products— cigarettes and chewing tobacco are examples—in spite of the health dangers.

The cycle of pollution also continues because of consumer habits. Few officials, for example, have been able to convince major portions of their cities' residents and commuters to share rides or use public transportation in order to cut down on the number of automobiles that jam the expressways and pollute the air with exhaust fumes.

Whatever the causes of increased environmental concerns, during the latter part of the 1980s the public once more called for cleanup of the air, water, and land. In addition, an emerging new issue was and still is *indoor pollution*. European scientists and EPA researchers in the United States found that air inside the home or workplace is often polluted by anywhere from 100 to 250 *volatile organic compounds* (VOCs)—those that easily change states (for example, changing from solid to gaseous state). Chemical concentrations indoors frequently reach levels that are two to five times higher and sometimes up to seventy times higher than federal standards would allow outdoors.

What are the sources of indoor pollutants? Air-conditioning systems, gas furnaces and stoves, insulation materials, home fireplaces, radiation (from radon gas), tobacco smoke, contaminated water and food, and a large number of consumer products, including carpets and furniture, may be the culprits.[1]

Exposure to a "chemical soup" in homes, schools, and workplaces can be a serious problem not only because pollutants are known toxins. Some also are difficult to detect. Many contaminants are odorless, tasteless, and invisible, and they provide little or no warning that they may be silent killers. The problem of such hazards is compounded by the fact that people spend 75 to 90 percent of their time indoors, and many buildings are tightly sealed to conserve energy.

When rooms are poorly ventilated, they also can become incubators for a variety of germs. Then, as air circulates, the bacteria and fungi spread about to do their dirty work. For example, germs can build up in heating and cooling systems, spreading infections such as lung ailments or the more serious illness Legionnaires' disease, named for a group of American Legion members who became ill while at a convention in Philadelphia in 1976. Legionnaires' disease is thought to be spread by bacteria that have spawned in air-conditioning systems. The disease sometimes results in pneumonia, which can be fatal, but it also can be cured with antibiotics.[2]

15

One safeguard against illnesses caused by "bad air" is making sure that heating and cooling systems and humidifiers are kept clean. But combating the menace of both indoor and outdoor pollutants is complex. Scientists are continually researching for ways to prevent dangers to public health.

Individuals also have to take responsible actions to protect themselves against air toxicity and other pollution hazards. Part of that process includes weighing the benefits of advances in technology—such as pesticide control and use of chemical fertilizers to improve agricultural production—against the potential hazards of toxic materials. Another part of the protective process is learning what substances can be silent killers and how to prevent health damage to yourself and others in the society. The chapters ahead provide some of that needed information.

2.
DIOXIN AND OTHER PERILS

The EPA has described dioxin as "one of the most perplexing and potentially dangerous chemicals ever to pollute the environment."[3] Dioxin and its chemical cousins are considered the most toxic substances ever manufactured. They are found in wood preservatives; in some paints, varnishes, adhesives, and soaps; and in a disinfectant called hexachlorophene. Dioxin was a component in waste oil used to control dust on roadways in Times Beach, Missouri, where twenty-four hundred people were evacuated in 1982–3 because of the dangers of exposure to the toxin.

Dioxin also is formed during combustion, and scientists in the United States and Europe are debating whether burning industrial and city wastes generates harmful amounts of dioxin. In February 1985, Sweden closed its garbage-burning plants in order to study the possible health hazards posed by incinerators and dioxin "fallout."

One study by Swedish chemist Christoffer Rappe, at the University of Umea, showed that emissions from incinerators were polluted with dioxin and contaminated land nearby. Cows grazing on the land produced milk with high levels of dioxin. Rappe's research group also found that people who live near incinerators may be absorbing dioxin. High levels

EPA inspectors, wearing protective clothing,
test soil in Times Beach, Missouri, for possible
dioxin contamination.

of dioxin—twenty to one hundred times above the level considered "safe"—were measured in human breast milk.[4]

DIOXIN COMPOUNDS

There are seventy-five different species, or chemical compounds, that are known as dioxins. A series of numbers identify individual compounds. For example, 2,3,7,8-tetrachlorodibenzo-p-dioxin, or TCDD, is the compound commonly known by the generic term *dioxin*. It is the most toxic. TCDD is produced with the manufacture of trichlorophenol, which in turn is used to make herbicides.

Dioxin compounds are so much a part of the industrial environment that some scientists believe the chemicals contaminate almost all people living in developed countries. This could result in a higher incidence of cancer in industrialized nations. However, no scientific studies have provided hard evidence that dioxin is a human carcinogen, or that human beings suffer serious long-term health effects from the chemicals.

Fred H. Tschirley, who "has spent many years studying the dioxin issue," wrote in an article for a February 1986 issue of *Scientific American* that "Many essentially acute symptoms [from dioxin exposure] have been observed in human beings. They include chloracne [a severe skin disease], digestive disorders, effects on some essential enzyme systems, aches and pains of muscles and joints, effects on the nervous system and psychiatric effects." He noted that the symptoms, "except for a few severe cases of chloracne," lasted for only a short time.

Yet, Tschirley also pointed out, as have many other researchers, that laboratory animals exposed to dioxin have developed several types of cancer, liver diseases, and birth defects. Such findings create great public concern that human beings will also suffer these long-term diseases because of dioxin exposure. But Tschirley contended that studies of people who have been exposed to high levels of TCDD (dioxin) show few, if any, chronic effects. As an example he pointed to workers in a Monsanto chemical company in West Virginia who were exposed to TCDD during an accidental spill at the plant. After the 1949 accident, 122 of the workers developed chloracne and all but one were monitored for the next thirty years. Wrote Tschirley:

> *The total number of deaths in that group did not differ significantly from that expected in the population at large, and there were no excess deaths due to cancer or diseases of the circulatory system. Similar findings have been made after other industrial accidents, except for two in which an excess of deaths from cancer was found in small groups of the people exposed.*[5]

"AGENT ORANGE"

Tschirley's findings would be disputed by many groups of veterans who served during the war in Vietnam. From 1962 to 1971, the U.S. military sprayed a herbicide called "Agent Orange," a potent form of TCDD, on millions of acres of land in Vietnam and Laos. The herbicide destroyed plant and tree foliage that provided ambush cover for enemy soldiers. In the years since the war, a number of U.S. veteran groups have contended that the defoliant has caused long-

A Vietnam War veteran stands on crutches outside the Federal Courthouse in Brooklyn, New York, in August 1984, during hearings on the harmful effects of Agent Orange.

term health problems, including several kinds of cancers, among those exposed.

In 1979, Congress ordered that studies be conducted on the effects of Agent Orange. One study, called the Ranch Hand study after a code name used by Air Force pilots in Vietnam, will be under way until 2002. The Ranch Hand study is comparing death rates of a group of veterans exposed to Agent Orange with those who were not exposed. So far there seems to be no higher rate of death from unusual causes among veterans exposed to dioxin.

Yet, other studies conducted by state agencies working with Vietnam veterans have found a correlation between various types of cancer and exposure to Agent Orange. In addition, studies of farmers who use herbicides made with the same chemicals found in Agent Orange have shown that dioxin is linked to diseases of the liver and cancer.[6] Scientists, however, continue to search for the evidence that will allow them to draw definite conclusions about dioxin's effects on humans.

CHLORDANE CONTROVERSY

Controversy also surrounds the health risks of chlordane, a chemical used to control termites and other insects. It is related to dichloro-diphenyl-trichloroethane (DDT), a pesticide that has been banned because it is known to cause cancer. Chlordane was widely used during the 1950s and 1960s in household insecticides but was replaced by other chemicals when chlordane became a suspected carcinogen and was blamed for other health problems such as nerve and reproductive damage. Some states have restricted the sale of chlordane to licensed exterminators, who use the chemical to prevent termites from traveling through soil to the foundation of homes.

When chlordane is used for termite control it is sprayed into the soil around the foundation of a house. Problems arise if chlordane fumes seep from the soil through heating and cooling ducts or through unsealed joints to the indoors.

Apparently that was how toxic fumes seeped into the home of an eastern couple who at first experienced flulike symptoms. Tests of the home showed high chlordane levels and the couple was forced to move out. However, the woman was pregnant at the time and later delivered a stillborn child. Doctors say the child appeared healthy in all ways but was contaminated with chlordane.

Many environmentalists and health researchers have warned that chlordane likely contributes to higher cancer rates, and EPA researchers have found that the chemical causes cancer in laboratory animals. The EPA announced in August 1987 that the pesticide would be banned—temporarily. However, EPA officials said that in order to prevent economic hardship, the agency will allow termite exterminators to use up their existing supplies of chlordane.

Meanwhile, the manufacturer, Velsicol Chemical Corporation, withdrew chlordane from the market to run tests in an attempt to prove to the EPA that the product is safe. If chlordane is applied properly, there is "nothing to worry about," company officials claim, insisting that none of their previous tests has shown chlordane to be a human health hazard.

Some exterminators also defend the use of chlordane. The president of a pest control company in Benton Harbor, Michigan, said he has had the chemical all over his body and in his clothes but is "in perfect health." However, other exterminators across the country, including those in states such as Indiana where chlordane can be sold over the counter, no longer use the product. Instead, exterminators are using chemical substitutes, such as dursban TC and pryfon, which are said to be safer but are more expensive and require more applications than chlordane.

METHYLENE CHLORIDE

You probably would not know the chemical by name, but methylene chloride is a common component in paint strippers, insecticides, and a variety of aerosol products such as

23

spray paints. However, it is not likely that a label on a container would tell you that methylene chloride is part of the contents. Rather, the manufacturer might use a term such as "chlorinated solvents" or "aromatic hydrocarbons," which covers a number of different chemicals.

Until recently, methylene chloride was widely used to decaffeinate coffee. Now, some food processors are careful to advertise that they are no longer using the chemical solvent as a decaffeination substance. Rather caffeine is removed from coffee and chocolate products by an agent that is "found naturally in such foods as bananas and apples."

Why did food processors make a shift? Perhaps because the results of laboratory tests show that methylene chloride causes numerous tumors in animals. It is also a suspected human carcinogen and thought to be a causative factor in nerve disorders and diabetes.

TOXIC EFFECTS
OF STYRENE

Another toxic chemical often found in homes and workplaces is styrene, used to make fiberglass, plastics, and synthetic rubber. During the mid-1980s, researchers in Italy studied a group of thirty women who worked in two fiberglass-boat factories and were exposed to high levels of styrene. A report on the findings of the Italian researchers was published in a 1986 edition of the *Boston Bulletin on Chemicals and Disease*, which summarizes scientific studies on the health effects of chemicals. As the *Bulletin* editors explained, for the first time a study showed "that occupational exposure to styrene causes profound hormonal changes in humans. The average length of exposure to styrene in these [Italian] workers was 6.2 years. . . ."

Researchers compared the women in the boat factories with the same number of other factory workers who were not exposed to styrene, and they found that styrene interferes with hormonal secretions and the body's ability to

24

regulate the central nervous system. According to the report, the effects of styrene were due to high concentrations of the chemical rather than exposure over long periods. Although the levels of styrene in the air of the Italian factories were more than two times higher than would be allowed in U.S. factories, the researchers believe this finding "may still be only of relative value." Persons sensitive to styrene may experience a toxic reaction to a buildup of the chemical in the body, the researchers concluded.

BENZENE: A
PROBABLE CARCINOGEN

Benzene is one more toxic chemical commonly used in American industry and found in dozens of consumer products. It is a component of cleaning solvents and paint removers. Although some people may be able to tolerate benzene fumes, those who cannot are likely to suffer headaches, nausea, or asthmatic-type symptoms from the chemical. If inhaled over long periods, benzene may cause leukemia.

Benzene levels are reportedly 30 to 50 percent higher in smokers' homes than in homes of nonsmokers.[7] When concentrations of the chemical are found indoors, they are measured, as are other air pollutants, by parts per million (ppm), billion (ppb), or trillion (ppt)—or the number of molecules of the pollutant mixed with a million (billion/trillion) molecules of air.

In the case of benzene, the Occupational Safety and Health Administration (OSHA) urged in 1985 that the standard of 10 ppm in workplaces be cut to 1.5-ppm exposure over an eight-hour workday. In September 1987, a new federal ruling required a 90 percent reduction of exposure to benzene on the job. As OSHA administrator John A. Pendergrass put it: "It has been proven beyond a doubt that benzene poses a significant risk of leukemia and other blood diseases to those exposed." He believes the lower limits will significantly reduce the number of deaths from leukemia among workers exposed to benzene during their occupational lifetime.

DANGERS OF CHLOROFLUOROCARBONS

Many urban residents have felt the effects of ozone, an air pollutant that triggers a number of respiratory problems. Ozone close to the ground can be a health hazard, but in the stratosphere, ozone forms a protective shield that surrounds the earth and filters out radioactive rays from the sun. Without ozone, life on earth as we know it would be destroyed. Thus, there has been widespread concern in recent years over the industrial use of a class of chemicals that could be depleting the ozone shield.

The chemicals are known as chlorofluorocarbons (CFCs), and in 1978 the U.S. government banned the use of CFCs in aerosol sprays. But manufacturers in other nations produce aerosols with CFCs, and industrial nations around the globe use the chemicals in making such products as refrigerators, air conditioners, electronic chips, and Styrofoam containers for fast-food restaurants.

In late 1987, one fast-food company, McDonald's, responded to a citizen campaign against the use of Styrofoam products and announced it would phase out its Styrofoam packaging in favor of paper wrappings that can be recycled. The McDonald's action was just a beginning step to eliminate CFC-produced goods on a worldwide basis. European countries produce almost half of the CFCs and the United States produces one-third. Late in 1987, officials from the United States and forty-five other nations met in Montreal, Canada, to sign an agreement to cut the use of CFCs by 50 percent over the next ten years. Developing nations will be exempt from CFC reductions for ten years because such actions would slow economic growth, officials say.

Some scientists have urged a more rapid reduction in

CFC use, warning that depletion of the ozone could lead to an increase in skin cancers, particularly among those who spend their leisure time relaxing and tanning in the sun. Many sunbathers believe that a tan "looks healthy" and thus must be a sign of good health. It is also fashionable for light-skinned people, who are more sensitive to ultraviolet radiation than dark-skinned people, to be tanned, and the so-called healthy look may seem more important than trying to prevent a skin disease later in life.

Melanoma is the most dangerous form of skin cancer. In 1930 only 1 American out of 1,500 developed melanoma. By 1986, there was a tenfold increase to 1 out of 150 people. One reason for the increase is longer life spans: melanoma has more opportunities to develop. The disease is expected to hit 1 out of every 100 persons in the United States by the year 2000, according to the American Cancer Society. To prevent melanoma and other types of skin cancer, experts recommend that people cover their skin, wear hats, and use sunscreens if they have to be outdoors and in the sun, especially during midday.[8]

DEBATE OVER FORMALDEHYDE

The use of formaldehyde in manufacturing has long been a matter of debate. In 1982, the federal Consumer Product Safety Commission banned urea-formaldehyde foam, an insulation material, because of its toxicity. As little as 0.1 ppm of formaldehyde in the air can create throat and lung irritation and sometimes serious health hazards. In some homes with the foam insulation, formaldehyde concentrations have measured 0.5 ppm, and in one Oakland, California, high school formaldehyde levels reached 1.45 ppm.

Consumer protection groups would like to see a complete ban or extremely limited use of urea-formaldehyde in all pressed-wood products. Toxic fumes escape from cabinets, floorboards, and other pressed-wood materials. Then the toxins are trapped inside many homes because home-owners have sealed up air leaks to cut energy costs. As a result, unless manufacturers of products containing formaldehyde reduce the emissions, many Americans "will continue to get sick without apparent reason and may run a higher risk of developing cancer," one consumer group has said. Some studies have shown that formaldehyde at fairly low levels does cause nasal cancers in laboratory animals.

In spite of the plea for protection from formaldehyde fumes, the federal courts in 1983 overturned the ban on urea-formaldehyde foam. Members of the court based their decision on arguments presented by business groups who questioned the evidence presented and claimed that only the EPA could rule on materials thought to be carcinogens.

The adverse publicity about urea-formaldehyde insulation has discouraged its use, but thousands of homes still contain the material as do up to three thousand building and household products, including some cosmetics, upholstery materials, carpeting, and permanent-press fabrics. Emissions from such products do tend to decrease over time. But exposure to the toxic fumes may be long term for people who live in mobile homes constructed with interior plywood and particle-board products.

One study, conducted by the Cancer Research Center in Seattle, Washington, and released for publication in 1986, showed "a strong and significant association between living in a mobile home for ten or more years and risk of nasopharyngeal cancer [a cancer of that part of the throat that leads to the nose]." However, researchers noted that before they could draw any definite conclusions, they would need to measure the concentrations of formaldehyde in mobile homes and also determine whether other factors may contribute to the high level of nasal cancers.

Manufacturers say that formaldehyde levels in homes produced since 1980 have dropped 65 to 90 percent. In addition, formaldehyde may become less of a health hazard when air is allowed to circulate freely in a mobile home or other building in which the chemical is emitting fumes.

3
ASBESTOS:
THOSE DEADLY FIBERS

Asbestos, like formaldehyde, has been a component in insulation materials and is a toxic substance. However, it is even more dangerous than formaldehyde, and some federal officials have called asbestos the most widespread toxic substance in the United States.

A natural mineral fiber found in rocks, asbestos has been used in construction since the time of ancient Rome. During the more recent past, manufacturers added the mineral to such building materials as patching compounds, textured paint, wrap for heating ducts and water pipes, insulation, floor and ceiling tiles, roofing shingles, and cement and plaster. Asbestos is also a component in vehicle brake linings and in a variety of other products. In fact, since the turn of the century, U.S. industries have used over 30 million tons of asbestos.

It is little wonder that asbestos has had widespread application in many industries. The mineral acts as an insulator and fire retardant; it strengthens concrete and sound-proofs; it allows for high traction and resists chemical breakdown. But in the 1950s, scientific studies of asbestos warned against possible hazards of lung disease from exposure to asbestos in manufacturing plants. By the 1960s, researchers found that the asbestos mineral fibers in aging building materials (such as insulation and ceiling tiles) can crumble and become airborne. The fibers may also be released from water pipes.

DANGERS OF ASBESTOS

Airborne asbestos fibers are like tiny glass slivers that can be inhaled, causing asbestosis, a disease that scars and stiffens the lungs. Asbestosis makes breathing difficult and impedes the supply of needed oxygen to the blood. Inhaled asbestos can cause lung cancer as well. According to the EPA, an estimated eight thousand to ten thousand deaths each year are the result of lung cancer brought on by asbestos exposure.

Asbestos is said to be bound or "locked into" cement that includes the mineral. But water running through asbestos-laced cement pipes can release the dangerous fibers. In the fall of 1985, for example, residents of Woodstock, New York, found that large quantities of fiber—in this case, blue-white fibers—were clogging pipe valves. In one instance, clumps of fiber fell on a woman who was showering.[9]

Alarmed citizens of Woodstock learned from private and state health officials that 80 percent of the fibers were a combination of two types of asbestos: "white" or chrysotile and "blue" or crocidolite asbestos. The latter has longer fibers and is considered more dangerous. (A third type of "brown" asbestos, amosite, is also more hazardous than chrysotile.)

Tests of the Woodstock water supply showed a total of more than 300 million fibers per liter of water, the highest count in New York State and in the top 1 or 2 percent for the nation. Although there is no positive proof that asbestos causes gastrointestinal cancer, evidence strongly suggests that asbestos ingested through water and food is related to cancers of the digestive system. High concentrations and long exposure to asbestos increase the risk of disease from the fibers.

WHO'S AT RISK?

Woodstock officials acted quickly to bypass the asbestos-cement pipes with a new water system for most of the community. (Removing the old pipes made with asbestos could have created even greater hazards since the crumbling cement might have caused asbestos fibers to be airborne.) Yet, no one can be sure just how much longtime residents of Woodstock have been endangered. Some may have been exposed to high concentrations of asbestos, and harmful effects—as with many other carcinogens—may not be known for many years.

Other towns and cities in the nation may be at risk because of asbestos-contaminated water. In communities of such diverse states as California, Connecticut, Florida, Virginia, and Minnesota, health officials have reported high asbestos fiber counts in water supplies.

Airborne asbestos, however, poses even greater and more widespread dangers. Approximately 25 million Americans could be victims of asbestos-related diseases, writes Paul Brodeur in his book *Outrageous Misconduct: The Asbestos Industry on Trial*. Many of the known victims who suffer from painful lung cancer were once construction or shipyard workers. They inhaled asbestos fibers while on the job during the 1940s and early 1950s. Family members—exposed to fibers in workers' clothing—are also potential victims.

Others potentially at risk are babies who have been exposed to asbestos. Researchers at the University of Texas in Galveston found that in autopsies of seventeen babies who died of sudden infant death syndrome (SIDS) or of an infectious disease, six had asbestos in their lungs. In a few, the levels of asbestos were as high as those of adults with mesothelioma, a cancer of the lungs.

31

Yet, researchers pointed out in their 1985 study that asbestos could not be considered a definite cause of SIDS. It may be possible, they noted, that those babies with asbestos in their lungs were more susceptible to the deadly mineral than other victims of SIDS.[10]

Patients confined for long periods in old hospitals and workers in aging public and private buildings are another group that may be endangered by asbestos exposure. The EPA surveyed just ten cities in the mid-1980s and found that 733,000 buildings contained asbestos. Nationwide, millions of old buildings with crumbling or deteriorating asbestos materials could be a threat to those who inhabit them.

One of the most alarming contamination problems is in old school buildings where wraps for boilers and ceiling tiles are the usual sources for asbestos. According to congressional reports, an estimated thirty-one thousand school buildings across the land may be contaminated with asbestos, endangering some 13 million students and about 2 million teachers and other school workers. Schoolchildren are at higher risk since they obviously are expected to live longer than adults and thus have greater chances of long-term exposure to deteriorating asbestos.

In the fall of 1986, Congress passed the Asbestos Hazard Emergency Response Act, which requires that local school districts develop laws for control or removal and disposal of asbestos, within guidelines set by the EPA. Congress allocated $100 million between 1984 and 1986 for the job.

Asbestos insulation is exposed on the ceiling of a hallway in a public school. This was one of two schools in the Harlem section of New York City that were closed because of parents' protests.

Then early in 1987, another $47.5 million in federal funds was provided for grants and loans to local school districts to help with high-priced asbestos cleanup projects. One Florida district expects to pay $10 million to remove asbestos from its schools.[11]

ASBESTOS IN THE HOME

In a number of national magazine articles and newspaper reports during recent years, writers have expressed grave concern over the possibility of asbestos materials in homes. Perhaps you have never suspected that any part of your home could contain toxic materials or that the air quality could pose a danger to your health. What are some telltale signs of asbestos hazards? How do people determine whether their living environment is contaminated?

One New York apartment dweller became suspicious of crumbling materials in a wooden cover for a radiator in her son's bedroom. A gray, powdery compound filled the wallboard-type material from which the cover had been made. Pieces of the compound had fallen on the floor. A lab test confirmed the woman's worst fears: The radiator cover contained chrysotile asbestos.

In other instances, tenants or home owners have found asbestos-filled wrapping for water pipes that may run through halls and laundry and storage rooms or may be around boilers in basements. Such a wrapping, which looks like corrugated cardboard or hardened plaster inside a protective covering, was commonly used in buildings constructed more than twenty-five to thirty years ago. Today, the wrappings may be dented, torn, or otherwise damaged or may be deteriorating from age. Residents of older buildings have also found acoustic ceiling tiles made of asbestos. These were often installed in basement recreation rooms and in family rooms until the 1970s.

What should you do if you suspect that some material

in your home is made of asbestos? If the material, such as shingles, insulation wrap, tiles, sprayed-on fireproofing that looks like matted upholstery stuffing, is in good condition, it may pose no hazard at the moment. The experts say that intact, undamaged asbestos should be left alone. Trying to remove it without expert help might release fibers into the air. But asbestos-containing materials that are friable—that is, that crumble easily—are a real and present danger because they may already be releasing deadly fibers into the air.

ASBESTOS CONTROL

One of the first steps in asbestos control or removal is to find out whether a suspected material is indeed toxic. Experts in environmental consultant agencies set up in major cities can survey a house or apartment, collect air or building material samples, and test those samples in their laboratories. However, the price tag for this on-site service may be between three hundred and five hundred dollars, which includes lab fees, travel time, and recommendation for dealing with asbestos (if it is present).

To save on the cost of a home survey, some people have chosen to collect their own samples and take them to a lab or environmental agency where fees for analysis are between thirty and forty dollars. Such a procedure can be done safely by the layperson if—and it is a big if—precautions are taken. For example, the EPA and the U.S. Consumer Product Safety Commission (CPSC) in Washington, D.C., say that a person should wear rubber gloves and a protective mask when picking up any asbestos materials.

It is also important to prevent asbestos from becoming airborne by dampening materials with a spray mister such as the type used for house plants. The samples should then be put into a heavy plastic bag or film canister to mail or deliver to a testing service. The EPA and the CPSC can supply names and addresses of testing companies that are qualified to analyze asbestos materials. The accepted method of analysis is called *polarized light microscopy*. Other methods, such as a chemical test of materials, are more likely to produce false results, the experts say.

Jointly, the EPA and the CPSC have also published a booklet entitled *Asbestos in the Home*, which can be obtained free by writing to the U.S. Consumer Product Safety Commission, 1111 18th Street N.W., Washington, D.C. 20207, or by calling the agency's toll-free number: 800-638-2772.

Among the helpful guidelines in the booklet are recommendations for the layperson who wants to take on minor repairs of damaged or deteriorating asbestos materials. An example of a minor repair job is sealing damaged pipe wrappings. However, precautions are still in order, and again the EPA and CPSC warn that a person needs to wear disposable protective clothing, including gloves, mask, throwaway coveralls, and rubbers. Materials to use for repairs are described in the booklet.

For major jobs—such as those that involve removing all asbestos materials from the home or other building, not just containing them—the EPA recommends that building owners consult a technical adviser. The adviser should be an industrial hygienist or a consultant recommended by a local or regional EPA office, a person who is independent of the contracting firm that may charge thousands of dollars for asbestos removal. If a contractor must be hired to remove asbestos, the EPA can provide guidelines for the types of qualifications a contractor should have.

REGULATING
ASBESTOS USE

Worldwide, many industrialized nations have banned the use of asbestos, particularly since the mineral was identified as a carcinogen. In 1979, the U.S. government, through the EPA, outlawed asbestos insulation and in early 1986 banned such products as asbestos felts used under floor and roofing tiles and pipe made with asbestos. But other products made with asbestos are still being manufactured and sold in the United States.

Brake linings, for example, continue to be manufactured from asbestos materials because federal government officials claim no "acceptable" substitute has been found for friction brake products. Engineers and designers of motor vehicles say that some semimetallic materials have been used in place of asbestos for front disk brakes. But the substitute materials provide less traction, and if used for rear drum brakes would necessitate that the brake be redesigned to meet government standards.

Still, the use of asbestos in the United States dropped from about 875,000 tons in 1973 to less than 200,000 in 1985. In addition, OSHA passed new regulations for the level of asbestos exposure permitted in manufacturing plants. The earlier exposure level had been set at 2 fibers per cubic centimeter of air. Now the permissible level is 0.2 fibers per cubic centimeter.

The EPA has also proposed a phaseout of nearly all asbestos use in the United States, which would include not only manufacturing and processing of asbestos but mining and importing of the mineral as well. Such a proposal has created political conflicts between Canada and the United States. Canada supplies most of the asbestos for the Western world, and a nearly complete U.S. ban on asbestos would be "quite a blow" to the Canadian economy, according to one official. Canadians fear that such an action by the United States would also be taken in other nations that follow U.S. technical practices and expertise. As a result, some Canadian officials have attempted to fight any widespread ban on asbestos, claiming that the hazards of asbestos exposure have been exaggerated, particularly those dangers related to asbestos in drinking water. There are also claims from

37

industry-sponsored researchers that some types of asbestos exposure may not be harmful.

South of the Canadian border, some U.S. officials have also been fighting a complete ban on asbestos. Indeed, the Office of Management and Budget (OMB) of the U.S. government secretly agreed to help the Canadians fight the ban. While publicly approving the EPA stand, the OMB delayed hearings on the proposal for two years. A congressional investigation in mid-1986 finally forced public disclosure of the proposed regulations for asbestos use. Supporters of an asbestos ban, such as building trade unions, environmental groups, and victims of asbestos-caused lung diseases, were able to make public their findings on the hazards of asbestos use and the need for strict regulations or an outright ban on use of the fiber.

4
DEATH BY ASPHYXIATION

In early spring of 1985, all five members of a New Jersey family were found slumped before the TV set—dead—in their home. No human intruder or foul play by any family member was to blame. However, the killer had been inside the home and had worked gradually and quietly. The family had never suspected they were in danger, but all died of asphyxiation.

The killer turned out to be carbon monoxide (CO), one of the most insidious and sometimes difficult-to-detect gases. It is produced by *incomplete combustion*, that is, the burning of fuels in areas with low levels of oxygen. On the other hand, *carbon dioxide* (CO_2) is the product of complete combustion, a chemical reaction that is necessary for the production of energy. Carbon dioxide, in fact, is produced by the combustion of cells in the body and is exhaled during breathing. The source of metabolic energy, CO_2 is quite different from the silent killer carbon monoxide.

The lethal effects of this colorless, odorless, and tasteless gas have long been known. In fact, the ancients often executed prisoners by exposing them to the smoke of wood fires. Today, it is not unusual to read or hear news accounts of accidental deaths or suicides caused by exhaust fumes from a vehicle motor.

Motor vehicle exhaust fumes are a primary source of carbon monoxide. But faulty heating systems can also produce the deadly gas. That was the case with the New Jersey family. A plugged vent in a natural-gas heating unit circulated the carbon monoxide fumes through their home, slowly producing its lethal effects. Although natural gas does not contain carbon monoxide, it produces carbon monoxide when it is burned in air with low levels of oxygen, such as when a furnace vent or flue is clogged.

THE GREAT IMITATOR

Just as the presence of carbon monoxide in a home or other building is sometimes difficult to identify, so is carbon monoxide poisoning sometimes difficult to diagnose. The gas is absorbed by the lungs. Poisoning occurs when carbon monoxide competes with oxygen in the bloodstream, reducing the amount of oxygen that reaches the heart, brain, and other vital organs. Sometimes exposure to carbon monoxide is acute and so are the symptoms of poisoning—a person may become disoriented, lose consciousness, and perhaps die. In other instances, poisoning is mild and symptoms may abate, particularly when a person leaves a closed area that is polluted with carbon monoxide.

People who suffer from mild carbon monoxide poisoning may appear to have the flu, a cold, or asthma or may even act drunk. Some may complain of weakness and fatigue over long periods. Others suffer from dizziness or blurred vision, and numbness or a tingling sensation in the toes and fingers. In short, carbon monoxide toxicity can be a great imitator. Its symptoms may be very similar to those exhibited by people with heart diseases, hypoglycemia (low blood sugar), or viral infections. As a result, doctors often misdiagnose carbon monoxide poisoning.

One woman on the East Coast, for example, spent months from December 1984 through March 1985 consulting doctors in an effort to find out what kind of "strange illness" she had.[12] At first it seemed she suffered from the flu, and the diagnosis appeared valid when her husband and two sons experienced the same symptoms: headaches, weakness, poor vision, and dizziness. However, the male members of the family appeared to recover whenever they left their home for school or work.

When the woman's symptoms continued through January of 1985, she made appointments with a variety of specialists ranging from an ophthalmologist to a gynecologist. None of the experts could find anything wrong with her and diagnosed her condition as "acute anxiety." It was a stroke of good fortune that led the woman to compare her condition to that of symptoms of carbon monoxide poisoning which she had read about in the local newspaper. That in turn prompted her to have the furnace in her home checked. It was leaking carbon monoxide through a cracked heat exchanger.

A Denver, Colorado, man approaching his seventies faced a similar situation a number of years ago. He stayed home from his job in a meat-packing plant, complaining of chest pains, chills, headache, and dizziness. But when the symptoms persisted, the man sought a second opinion and was told he was suffering the side effects of his diabetes and high blood pressure.

A few days later, the Denver man was in the hospital emergency room with dizziness, heart palpitations, and nausea. Still the symptoms seemed to indicate that he was suffering the side effects of his chronic health problems, and he was released from the hospital. But within four more days, he was in the emergency room once more with all the symptoms of a heart attack, including severe chest pains. Finally, laboratory tests showed that his blood contained high amounts of carboxyhemoglobin and low levels of oxygen. He was suffering from CO poisoning caused by a rusted flue for the gas furnace in his home. The man's wife had even higher levels of carboxyhemoglobin in her blood.

DIAGNOSING CO POISONING

Hemoglobin in the blood carries oxygen, but when carbon monoxide is inhaled it displaces the oxygen, adheres to the hemoglobin, and produces carboxyhemoglobin. Thus, the hemoglobin cannot carry a sufficient amount of oxygen from the lungs to body cells and tissues. High levels of carboxy-hemoglobin alert doctors to the possibility of carbon monoxide toxicity.

Yet, blood tests and other lab work, such as an electro-cardiogram (ECG), do not always suggest poisoning by carbon monoxide. In a report published in a 1983 issue of a medical journal, J. Douglas White, M.D., of Georgetown University Hospital, Washington, D.C., pointed out that the wide variety of symptoms associated with carbon monoxide poisoning "can be bewildering even to the experienced physician." He noted, for example, that in one study of Los Angeles heart patients, 40 percent experienced ECG changes because of moderate exposure to carbon monoxide (from exhaust fumes) during rush-hour traffic.[13]

Dr. White also explained, "Skin color is not a reliable indicator of the presence or severity of poisoning," as has been commonly assumed by the medical profession for many decades. "It is now recognized that the appearance of a cherry-red coloration of the skin, mucous-membranes, lips and nailbeds, widely believed to be characteristic, is rarely found" in patients who later die of carbon monoxide poisoning. Dr. White suggested that a physician should consider not only clinical symptoms but results of psychometric testing if carbon monoxide poisoning is suspected. As he explained: "Memory, psychomotor, and cognitive skills are diminished at surprisingly low levels [of carboxyhemoglobin in the blood]. . . ." Thus poor results on psychometric tests may indicate exposure to carbon monoxide.

TREATMENT

During the mid-1980s, several major U.S. magazines carried stories about victims of carbon monoxide poisoning. In each case, a rusted or clogged vent to a water heater or furnace caused carbon monoxide fumes to back up into a home, poisoning those living inside. All of the victims had had close calls with death, but their stories had happy endings since they not only lived to tell their tales but suffered no serious aftereffects.

If a person becomes disoriented or passes out as a result of carbon monoxide exposure, emergency treatment with an oxygen mask may be required. In less severe poisonings, the traces of gas may leave a person's system within six to twelve hours—if that person leaves the area containing carbon monoxide.

For example, all members of a family may be exposed to a carbon monoxide leak in their home, but perhaps only one person spends the greater part of the day inside. Those who work outside or away from the home may find that such symptoms as headache, dizziness, nausea, and fatigue disappear as soon as they leave the polluted area. The person who spends the greater part of the day exposed to carbon monoxide is of course most likely to be in the greatest danger.

CO IN CIGARETTE SMOKE

As is well known, cigarette smokers face high risks of heart disease and lung cancer, and "passive smokers"—nonsmokers who inhale others' smoke—face similar health hazards. In recent years, another potential health hazard of cigarette smoke has been identified. Carbon monoxide, which is a major component in cigarette smoke, may cause "learning and memory deficits in a developing fetus," according to a 1984 report on a laboratory study of animals.[14]

Certain physical defects such as low birth weight and

43

*Carbon monoxide, a major component of
cigarette smoke, is suspected of causing
brain damage in a developing fetus.*

premature birth have been linked for some time with cigarette smoke. Although the recent findings cannot yet be applied directly to humans, the researchers theorize that pregnant women who smoke probably pass on carbon monoxide to the fetuses in their wombs. The toxic gas may cause learning defects in their children.

The potentially high carbon monoxide content of cigarette smoke—42,000 ppm in some cases—is especially dangerous for skin divers, according to the publisher of *Skin Diver* magazine. In a June 1986 editorial, the publisher pointed out that 100 ppm of carbon monoxide in the air is considered dangerous for the average person and "anything more than 10 parts per million is dangerous" for scuba divers.

He further explained that if a person has smoked before diving, the carbon monoxide reduces the amount of oxygen flowing through the blood, and that the reduction "can be one of the most serious problems facing a diver."

"To complicate matters, we find that effects of carbon monoxide absorption are surprisingly long lasting. It takes the body six hours to reduce the level of carbon monoxide by 50 percent, and traces of this contaminant can remain for twenty-four hours or more. If divers want to completely purge their bodies of carbon monoxide for a dive trip, they should not take a puff for at least two days prior to the event, and abstain from smoking until six hours after the dive, so that decompression functions [allowing the air pressure to return to normal] can go on unhampered," the publisher advised.

GUARDING AGAINST ASPHYXIATION

You know immediately when you are exposed to cigarette smoke, but how can you guard against exposure to carbon monoxide from other sources? Knowing the symptoms brought on by this deadly gas is a first step toward identifying a possible carbon monoxide leak.

45

A second, major preventive step is making sure that a building has proper ventilation, a serious problem in many structures, especially those that have been remodeled or recently constructed. In times past, drafty houses or other buildings with high ceilings and steam or hot-water heat posed less risk of carbon monoxide poisoning. Deadly fumes could escape. However, during the 1970s, many building owners "buttoned up" their property to conserve on fuel. They installed new insulation, storm windows, weather stripping, and other sealants to make their buildings airtight.

New buildings usually are tightly constructed and depend on ventilating or air-exchange systems to circulate air. If the ventilating system breaks down or does not work properly, there may be risks from trapped fumes or other contaminants, especially if, as in some offices and schools, there are no windows or the windows will not open to vent unwanted fumes.

In an airtight building or small space, it is wise to check that vents, flues, or chimneys for any type of combustion unit are open and free of obstructions. Kerosene or charcoal stoves, fireplaces, water heaters, and furnaces in your home should all be vented properly. If you suspect incomplete combustion in a stove or heating system, you can check the flame. It should be blue. An orange or yellow flame may be a sign that carbon monoxide is being produced.

A heating service worker should also inspect flues and chimneys periodically—once a year if possible. If flues and chimneys are clogged with soot or other debris they should be cleaned so that toxic fumes can escape.

5
RADON:
THE "NEW" POLLUTANT

Until the mid-1980s, the general public had little knowledge of radon, another type of colorless, odorless, and toxic gas. Unlike carbon monoxide, however, radon is not produced by combustion or human activities. Rather, it is a gas that occurs naturally as part of the decay process of uranium ore in rocks and soils. The by-products of the gas are radioactive, and those exposed to indoor radon may risk developing lung cancer. Outside, radon disperses quickly, so it is seldom a health hazard.

Swedish researchers had discovered high levels of radon in much of their housing built early in the 1970s. The gas came from concrete made with alum shale, which has high concentrations of uranium. After the Swedish discovery, American scientists and those in other countries were alerted to look for radon pollutants indoors.

In the United States, indoor radon contamination was found in such diverse states as Maryland, Florida, Illinois, and Colorado. Since a relatively small number of homes were tested, and there was no widespread publicity about the problem, radon did not appear to be a national menace. Then the experience of Stanley Watras made the news wire services.

SOUNDING THE ALARM

An engineer at a nuclear power plant near Boyertown, Pennsylvania, Stanley Watras gained national attention in December 1984. One afternoon he was ready to leave his job as usual but most unexpectedly set off radiation monitors (devices similar to metal detectors at airport gates). It was rare for anyone at the nuclear plant to come into contact with radioactive materials. Even more unusual was the fact that Watras triggered the plant monitors every afternoon for nearly two weeks. So each day he had to spend hours in the contamination room to allow the radioactivity to decay to safe levels before he could leave.

With plenty of time to think about his predicament, Watras concluded that the radioactivity was not work-related but probably had some connection with his home. He tested his idea one morning by going directly from his suburban, split-level house to the plant radiation monitors, rather than into any work areas where there might be radioactivity. Like a TV game show winner, he hit the "jackpot." The buzzers went off and the red light flashed. But the only "prize" Watras won was the assurance that experts in radiation measurement would check out his home.

MEASURING RADON

The standard measure for radioactivity is a *curie*, and experts record concentrations of radon in a unit called a *picocurie* (pCi). These are usually expressed on the basis of a liter of water or air as pCi/*l*. Another type of radon measurement is the *working level*, which represents the amount of energy released as the gas radioactively decays. This measurement is expressed in *working levels* (WL) with 1 WL equal to about 200 pCi/*l*.

In the Watras case, officials called in from the Pennsylvania Department of Environmental Resources (DER) found the house contaminated with radioactive radon gas. Radon concentrations measured from about 8 WL in the bedrooms to 16 WL in the living room and as high as 22 WL in the basement. In all parts of the dwelling, concentrations of radon were many times higher than the safety level allowed for uranium miners, a group with a high incidence of cancer linked to radon exposure.

On a yearly basis, family members who spent most of their time in the home—Watras's wife and young children—could be exposed to radiation more than one hundred times the level considered safe in uranium mines. Putting it another way, the risk from radon exposure was equivalent to the health hazard associated with smoking from 135 to over 200 packs of cigarettes a day.

Alarmed DER officials advised the Watras family to leave their home. They moved into a motel until the experts could determine how to reduce the radiation levels.

Meantime, the DER surveyed homes of the Watrases' neighbors and found extensive radon contamination, although none of the dwellings reached the levels of the Watras home. The survey was expanded to include over two thousand homes in the townships surrounding Boyertown. By late summer 1985, the Boyertown area was on its way to becoming known as the nation's "hot spot" of radon contamination.

SOURCES OF RADON

Although radon gas is radioactive, it in itself is not the major hazard. Instead, in the uranium and radium decay process radon continues to break down and produces stable isotopes called *radon daughters*. These can be inhaled directly or along with dust or other particles in the air. Then the radon products can decay in the lungs, irradiating healthy tissues and causing formation of cancer cells.

Radon daughters may also be ingested through drinking water that has been contaminated by the gas, perhaps causing leukemia and other cancers. Radon may seep from soils

49

into private wells or small community water systems. However, it is seldom a problem in city water systems because the gas is usually released into the air before it reaches consumers. According to the EPA, "Radon in water can be released into the air when the water is agitated, aerated, or heated."

Geologists say that small deposits of uranium can be found in all areas of the United States, but the sources of radon vary from state to state. Large concentrations are found in Pennsylvania, including the cities of Allentown and Reading, plus the New Jersey highlands and adjacent southern New York. This region, known as the Reading Prong, is actually only a small part of a geologic formation in the United States that is made up of volcanic rocks such as soft granite. The rocks and surrounding soils have unusually high deposits of uranium.

A similar situation exists in western states such as Colorado, Wyoming, Idaho, and Montana, with Colorado showing the highest levels of radon in homes, according to an EPA report issued in August 1987. The EPA also noted that black shale areas in central and southern Indiana and in Tennessee pose a high risk of radon contamination.

Some Florida residents have to worry about radon as well. Millions of acres of land in the state contain phosphate that is laced with uranium. Some of the uranium-rich phosphate soils pose more of a hazard than others, however.

This map, issued by the EPA, shows areas of the country where radon is suspected of existing in health-threatening amounts, but other factors must also be considered, such as soil type and permeability and housing type.

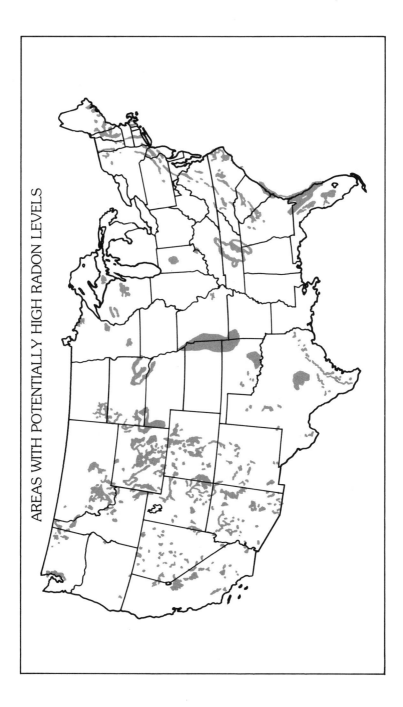

AREAS WITH POTENTIALLY HIGH RADON LEVELS

When the uranium in the phosphate is deep in the soil, the radon decay products usually stay within the earth. But phosphate that is near the surface may be mined or disturbed by construction projects, allowing radon to escape and become trapped inside homes and other buildings.

HOW RADON ENTERS BUILDINGS

Since radon is a gas it can seep through small spaces between rocks and percolate through soil. Homes or other buildings constructed on land formations that produce radon are susceptible to gas seepage as well. Radon can leak through cracks in a concrete foundation or cement blocks, through joints of buildings, through dirt in a crawl space under a building, and through floor drains. Usually, people living in one- or two-story homes are more likely to be exposed to radon than those living in apartment buildings. Tests have shown that radon levels in high-rise structures are somewhat lower because there is less contact with the ground per cubic meter of living space.

Yet, homes built on similar land formations that contain uranium do not necessarily have similar concentrations of radon. Even houses that are side by side or nearby in a neighborhood may not share the same levels of radon contamination. How is this possible?

One of the best explanations comes from physicist Anthony Nero, an internationally known expert on radon who heads a research group at the University of California's Lawrence Berkeley Laboratory. In a 1986 article for *Technology Review*, Nero pointed out that in their initial radon research, the Berkeley group followed the example of Swedish researchers whose investigation had found concrete to be a major source of radon. However, the California researchers examined "about a hundred samples of concrete" from across the United States and concluded that these materials accounted for only a small portion of radon pollution indoors.

"While investigating the properties of concretes, our group had also begun to examine the connection between indoor concentrations of radon and ventilation rates," Nero continued. "This was based on a second false premise: that tightening buildings to save energy would have a large influence on whether a house had high radon levels."

The theory that airtight buildings have contributed significantly to indoor radon pollution has been repeated a number of times in news stories published nationwide since the mid-1980s. But after measuring radon concentrations and ventilation rates in houses, the Berkeley physicists "found little or no correlation between the two." In fact, some drafty houses had levels of radon as high as or higher than those of tightly sealed houses. "We were forced to conclude that differences in the radon levels in various homes were primarily due to differences in the strength of the radon source," Nero wrote.[15]

Further tests showed that houses pull radon from the earth because of pressure differences between indoor air and air pressure in the soil. If the pressure of radon gas in the bedrock or soil is greater than the air pressure inside a house, the gas can be drawn indoors through small openings. The researchers have concluded that low indoor air pressure is one of the most important factors in determining the levels of radon concentration in a house.

RADON DETECTION

The EPA and research groups, such as the one at Lawrence Berkeley Laboratory and the physicists with the Radon Project under the direction of Dr. Bernard Cohen at the University of Pittsburgh, have been testing ways to prevent or reduce indoor radon pollution. Tests are still going on, and researchers emphasize that investigations and studies are far from complete. They also stress that no two houses are exactly alike nor are the soils beneath them.

Another important point is the fact that the vast majority

*Removing radioactive soil from under and
near homes in Montclair, New Jersey*

of homes in the United States are free of radon problems. However, up to 8 million homes may have radon levels high enough to warrant taking action to reduce radon concentrations. So how are these homes identified?

In some areas of the nation known to have high concentrations of radon-producing bedrock and soils, the state or local governments are carrying out testing services and providing radon detectors for residents. Also, the EPA has authorized several university laboratories and private businesses to conduct radon testing in various parts of the nation. For example, you can write to Dr. Bernard Cohen, Department of Physics, University of Pittsburgh, Pittsburgh, PA 15260. For a twelve-dollar check payable to the University of Pittsburgh you can get a radon detector (made of activated charcoal) which will absorb any radon in your home. The container must be returned along with a completed questionnaire to the University, where scientists will measure the radon absorbed by the charcoal. Not only will you receive an estimate of radon levels in your home, but you will also contribute to a radon research project.

Other approved testing services include the following:

Radon Testing Corporation of America
12-C West Main Street
Elmsford, New York 10623
(800) 457-2366

Terradex Corporation
3 Science Road
Glenwood, Illinois 80425-1679
(312) 755-7911

Maine State Department of Human Services
Public Health Lab Station 12
221 State Street
Augusta, Maine 04333
(207) 289-2727

New Jersey Department of Environmental Protection
Environmental Labs Administration
380 Scotch Road
Trenton, New Jersey 08628
(609) 530-4100

University of Illinois
Environmental Research Lab
1006 West Western Avenue
Urbana, Illinois 61801
(217) 333-6230

Radiation Safety Engineering Incorporated
7713 South Butte Avenue
Tempe, Arizona 85284
(602) 897-9459

Radon Measurement and Services
13131 West Cedar Drive
Lakewood, Colorado 80220
(303) 980-5086

Researchers use a number of sophisticated sampling devices to detect radon in buildings. But for the layperson, two types of radon detectors are common. One is the type you can request from the Radon Project at the University of Pittsburgh. It may be a pouch or can containing activated charcoal or carbon that will absorb radon and hold its decay products. The other is an alpha track detector made of plastic. Alpha particles from the radon decay process hit the plastic and produce tracks that can only be seen under a microscope.

Radon measurements should be taken in the lowest livable section of your home, such as the basement. The area should be closed off for the screening period, which could range from a few days to several weeks.

Once the screening is completed, the results will determine what the health risks might be. Radon levels above 0.02 WL (or 4 pCi/l) are considered hazardous. Assuming that people spend between 75 and 80 percent of their time indoors, 4 pCi/*l* of indoor radon exposure over a lifetime of about seventy years could result in one to five deaths from lung cancer per one hundred persons. At a radon dose of 20 pCi/*l* between six and twenty-one out of one hundred people will die of lung cancer; 200 pCi/*l* concentrations result in between forty-four and seventy-seven cancer deaths per hundred persons. If the length of exposure drops, the lung cancer death rates drop accordingly. For example, at 100 pCi/*l* over a ten-year period, the rate is estimated to be between fourteen and forty-two lung cancer deaths per hundred.

How can you cut your risks if results of radon screening are high? Of course, the best measure is to eliminate or reduce radon in a home. But how soon must residents take action? EPA recommends using these guidelines:

MEASUREMENT	WHAT TO DO
1.0 WL (200 pCi/*l*) or higher	Reduce radon levels within several weeks; may need to relocate temporarily
0.1 to about 1.0 WL (20 to about 200 pCi/*l*	Reduce levels below 0.1 WL (20 pCi/l) within several months
0.02 to about 0.1 WL (4 pCi/*l* to about 20 pCi/*l*)	Reduce levels below 0.02 WL (4 pCi/l) if possible; act within several years
0.02 WL or lower (4 pCi/*l* or lower)	About average for homes; difficult to reduce levels

If there is a high level of radon in your home and you cannot reduce it quickly, you and your family can still take some immediate actions to lower your risks of lung cancer. For one thing, you can spend less time in areas of your home with high radon concentrations. Smoking may increase a person's risk to radon and definitely raises the overall risk of lung cancer, so another important action

57

would be to persuade smokers in your home to stop or cut back on smoking.

RADON REDUCTION

A number of nationally distributed magazines have carried illustrated instructions on how to reduce radon in a home. Such information usually has been adapted or excerpted from booklets published jointly by the EPA and the U.S. Centers for Disease Control (CDC). You can request the booklets from your regional EPA office or state radiation protection agency.

One of the methods for radon reduction is covering exposed earth (as in a crawl space) with cement. Another is sealing porous walls and cracks in concrete, cement blocks, and openings at building joints and around pipes. Wall and floor surfaces usually have to be carefully prepared for sealants such as waterproof paints and epoxy. Sealing materials also have to be gas-proof and nonshrinking. In addition, every opening has to be sealed for this method to work.

Sometimes radon is reduced by ventilating a basement or crawl space, the area closest to the soil, which is a primary source of radiation. Houses that sit on concrete slabs can be ventilated by opening windows around all levels of the house. But experts caution against reducing air pressure within the house since this is one of the factors that help draw radon indoors. "To guard against this, be certain to open vents or windows equally on all sides of the house. Also, minimize the use of exhaust fans," the EPA advises.

Forced ventilation using a fan to bring air from outdoors into a basement and pushing gas-laden air out through open windows is another common radon reduction method. But there is a danger that more radon may be drawn into a house.

Sometimes drastic measures must be taken, such as

installing a system of pipes through the concrete slab foundation and using fans to draw radon from the house to the outside. In other instances, drain tiles may have to be installed around a house, with fans to suck radon from the tiles. Such measures can cost thousands of dollars.

Whatever the methods required, performing accurate tests and hiring qualified contractors are important parts of any effort to reduce radon in the home effectively. The best way to locate a competent and reasonably priced specialist in radon reduction is to get in touch with a state radiation protection agency. Or an EPA regional office can help. Even with an expert's estimate of costs for radon reduction, a second opinion may be helpful. In some states, health officials may be able to determine whether proposed costs are reasonable.

6
DANGEROUS METALS

Toxic gases and fumes. Poisonous chemicals. Cancer-causing fibers. Now add dangerous metals to the list of silent health hazards. Although small amounts of some metals, such as iron, copper, manganese, and zinc, are needed by the body, other metals, such as mercury and lead, are health threats—even in trace amounts.

A century ago, it was not unusual for people to be exposed to toxic metals in their homes and workplaces. During the 1800s, London hatmakers, for example, inhaled mercury fumes, and as a result many suffered mental and nervous disorders. They twitched and trembled, exhibiting behavior that earned them an unflattering distinction: They became known as "mad hatters."

Since the 1970s in the United States, cases of mercury and lead poisoning have seemed to diminish. The public became more aware of sources of these deadly metals and used more protective measures, and some industries cut back on the use of mercury and lead. Today, however, the problem of poisoning from these metals still persists—at far too high a level, according to some observers. An increasing number of people are exposed to mercury and lead through contaminated water supplies and sometimes because manufacturers do not protect their employees from known dangers of these toxins.

MERCURY POISONING

One source of mercury poisoning is dimethyl mercury, an organic mercury compound produced by some microorganisms. Scientists learned about the toxic effect of the compound in 1953 when more than forty people in Japan died and dozens became ill after eating fish contaminated with dimethyl mercury. The fish came from waters polluted with elementary mercury from a nearby chemical plant.

Since the 1953 tragedy, similar cases, although not of the magnitude of those in Japan, have occurred in other parts of the world, including the United States. In 1970, fish caught in Lake Erie were found to contain high levels of dimethyl mercury due to industrial discharges of mercury into the waters.

Inorganic mercury, or mercury vapors, can also be toxic. In a "classic" case—one that is like a textbook description— of poisoning from mercury vapors, a person may suffer from dizziness and trembling; twitching muscles; clumsiness; chronic fatigue; forgetfulness; periods of depression and antisocial behavior; and sore and bleeding gums and loose teeth.

Such symptoms were described by a woman who worked in a Missouri chemical laboratory. During three years on the job, her health steadily deteriorated until her doctor found high levels of mercury in her blood and treated her for mercury poisoning. She had never been warned about mercury dangers in the workroom, where vapors were embedded in walls and floors.

Mercury vapors are a hazard in many laboratories, including school chemistry labs. If mercury spills, it should be collected in the proper laboratory receptacle—a tube that sucks up and traps the material. But spilled drops can collect

61

in tiny cracks of wall, floor, and table surfaces, and emit harmful vapors. Once inhaled, mercury enters the bloodstream and over a period of time can damage the brain and nervous system.

Chemistry students are warned about the dangers of vapors from spilled mercury, even mercury that may come from a broken thermometer. Also, an increasing number of industrial workers have become aware of mercury hazards and ways to avoid them, thanks to efforts of the National Institute for Occupational Safety and Health (NIOSH). NIOSH has published recommendations and standards for controlling exposure to inorganic mercury, or vapors from mercury. However, not all workers can read or understand the NIOSH guidelines. And some employers neglect—sometimes on purpose—to inform their employees of dangerous toxins in the workplace.

Such a charge was leveled at the owners of Pymm Thermometer in Brooklyn, New York, where more than half the eighty to one hundred employees were found to be contaminated with mercury in 1984. Several died of mercury poisoning. Most of the workers were and still are poor blacks and Hispanics.

Grisly details of how the Pymm workers have long been exposed to mercury vapors were carefully outlined in a major feature published in a 1987 issue of *The Progressive* magazine. According to the authors of the feature, the Pymm brothers, who own the thermometer plant, were indicted by a New York grand jury in October 1986 and charged with "assault for allegedly endangering the lives of workers by knowingly and continually exposing them to mercury."[16]

Court watchers familiar with corporate cases say the odds are strongly against conviction of the Pymm brothers. Only one other similar case has resulted in a conviction of corporate officials who deliberately exposed workers to toxic substances. That case involved the Film Recovery Systems Corporation in a Chicago suburb where a worker died of cyanide poisoning and many others became ill. A sodium cyanide solution was used in the Film Recovery plant to extract valuable silver from used X-ray film. But the workers, who were Polish and Mexican immigrants, were not aware of the hazards of the cyanide fumes or the sludge that could be absorbed through the skin. The skull-and-crossbones symbols that once marked containers of poisonous materials had been painted over. In addition, none of the workers received the proper gloves or masks for protection, and there were no windows or fans in the warehouse-type building where the silver recovery took place.

After the death of the plant worker in March 1983, five company officials were indicted by a grand jury for murder. Three were convicted of manslaughter in 1985. It was the first time in the United States that company officials were held accountable for deliberately endangering the lives of their employees.

ANOTHER MERCURY PROBLEM?

For the past decade or so, there has been an ongoing debate about the dangers of another type of exposure to mercury. Although the problem may not be life-threatening, it does raise serious questions about the health hazards of dental fillings that contain mercury. Yes, dental fillings.

For at least 150 years dentists have used so-called silver amalgams to fill a tooth cavity after decay has been removed. Silver amalgams, however, are really an alloy of metals in a solution of mercury (which is what *amalgam* means). Thus "silver" fillings are only 30 percent silver; plus some copper, tin, and zinc; and about 50 percent mercury.

It is the toxic mercury in fillings that has caused controversy in the dental profession. Although it was commonly believed that mercury was "locked in" and vapors could not leak out of fillings, some researchers today are convinced that with chewing or breakdown of filling materials mercury vapors do indeed seep out, and particles of toxic metal may

63

also enter the body. Such mercury leaching over a period of years may bring about adverse health effects, including nerve disorders, allergies, and gastrointestinal problems. Dentists convinced of the toxic effects of mercury fillings say that many health problems disappear when mercury fillings are removed.

Critics of this theory point out that nearly all of us ingest some mercury if we consume various seafoods, some medications, or alcohol, or are exposed to cigarette smoke. However, a person excretes mercury through urine, although no one is sure just how much stays in the body and how much buildup of the toxic metal may occur over a long period.

The American Dental Association (ADA) maintained in 1984 that only "individuals sensitive to mercury" had any reason to be concerned about the toxicity of silver fillings. ADA officials point out as well that no scientific studies on the effects of mercury in fillings show them to be a health hazard.

An increasing number of dentists, however, do not accept the ADA position and believe there have been enough findings on mercury toxicity to warrant using substitute materials for fillings.[17] One substitute is a gold alloy that has been in use for many years, but its price and quality fluctuate, depending on the base metals used. Another substitute is a metal-free composite of materials called *bonded resin ceramics*, which has been in use since the 1960s.

Since there are no clear-cut answers on the possible dangers of mercury-based dental fillings, the issue will probably continue to stir controversy. Unfortunately patients who may suffer the effects of mercury poisoning have few opportunities to learn about both sides of the argument, unless they can consult the scientific literature on the subject or talk to various dentists with different points of view. So if you are concerned about mercury in your dental fillings, probably your first move should be to open your mouth—to ask questions, lots of them.

NO PLACE FOR LEAD

No great mystery or controversy surrounds the subject of the heavy metal lead. It does not belong in the body and is highly toxic. Even low levels of lead can cause chronic digestion problems, hearing loss, and stunted growth. Pregnant women who ingest lead risk bearing children with mental and physical disabilities. Lead toxicity in middle-aged men can cause hypertension, heart attacks, and strokes.

Yet, a good many of us carry around low levels of lead and unknowingly may be ingesting this toxic metal—in spite of the fact that the amount of lead in the environment has been dropping, particularly since the phaseout of lead gasoline began during the 1970s. (Lead was commonly used as a gasoline additive to prevent engine "knocking.")

The metal still can be found in millions of older homes with lead-based paint and caulking. Although such lead-based materials are now outlawed, they are a major cause of poisoning in young children, who are more susceptible to the toxin than are adults. Youngsters absorb lead quickly and store the toxin in fluids and soft tissues, where damage can be extensive. The children in poor, urban families are especially at risk since they often live in substandard housing where lead in paint chips and crumbling mortar can contaminate homes.

The New York University Medical Center warned recently that some children in art classes risk ingesting lead from art supplies. Although lead is banned in household paint, it is permissible in art materials. According to an art therapist at the University's rehabilitation center, "Lead is incorporated in many types of paints, ceramic glazes and solder used for stained-glass windows." The therapist emphasized that children under twelve should not use art materials with lead, and that all creative play materials for younger children should be checked to be sure they are nontoxic.

Some industrial workers may also be at risk as a result of exposure to high levels of lead in the workplace. In July 1987, for example, OSHA cited and fined Chrysler Corporation for allowing high levels of lead and arsenic compounds in soldering and paint booth areas of its auto assembly plant in Newark, Delaware. Company officials said they immediately took steps "to improve the monitoring of the booths [for toxins] and employees that work there."

"LEADED" DRINKING WATER

An even larger group of Americans may be at risk because of lead in drinking water. In late 1986, the EPA issued a report showing that 42 million of us may be consuming high levels of lead with our tap water.[18] The EPA set the safety level for lead in drinking water at 50 parts per billion (ppb), dropping to 20 ppb by mid-1988.

Of those Americans who are exposed to lead-contaminated water, very few realize they are at risk. Lead in water is invisible, tasteless, and odorless, so certified lab technicians have to test the water to determine whether it is lead-free.

Usually, lead in drinking water is discovered only after it causes health problems. However, with increased awareness of the possibility of the presence of lead in drinking water, more and more consumers are having their water tested. In addition, the EPA has identified a number of "hot spots" in the nation where lead contamination is a problem. States

Children at play in a New York City slum. Children who live in substandard housing, with peeling lead paint, and crumbling mortar, are at risk.

67

with "soft" water—that is, acidic water low in dissolved minerals—tend to have high lead levels. Soft water usually leaches metal from lead pipes and from the solder that joins copper pipes.

Unless lead-free plumbing is used, the pipes in newer homes are more likely to produce contaminated water than those in older homes. Why? Because most of the lead corrosion in pipes takes place the first few years, then mineral deposits may coat and seal the pipes, reducing the amount of lead contamination.

Some city water systems may also have high levels of lead. To overcome the problem, suppliers can treat the soft water by adding soda or lime, which cuts down on the acidity and makes it less corrosive. Some municipal water companies also are replacing old pipes with lead-free systems.

REDUCING LEAD HAZARDS

Of course, the best way to eliminate the hazard of lead-contaminated water is to remove the toxin. However, removing the lead source may be too expensive or beyond your control. So as a precaution you may want to use bottled water for drinking or cooking. Before using water from the tap, turn on the faucet for several minutes to flush out lead that may be in pipes. Do not use hot tap water for cooking since it is more likely to leach lead.

Whether or not lead is in your drinking water, you cannot avoid it in other areas of your living environment. Lead can be found in the air, in some soils, and in foods. But you can reduce the risk of lead contamination in a number of ways.

1. Avoid storing or cooking food in clay-type dishes and other earthenware containers that have not been approved for such purposes. Lead can seep from glazes that have been improperly fired. Most ceramic products made in the United States are safe, but some imports may not be.

2. If you open a fruit-juice can, do not store the unused portion in the open can in the refrigerator. Lead may be leached from the solder in the can. Put the leftover juice into a glass jar or plastic container.

3. Warn young children to stay away from building areas where remodeling is under way. In such areas, youngsters may be exposed to lead-laden paint chips or dust particles.

4. To reduce the toxic effects that lead contamination can have, eat foods high in calcium and zinc. These include dairy products, fish, and green vegetables. (Studies have shown that undernourished children absorb lead faster and suffer more damage than those who eat a nutritious diet.)

5. Finally, if you suspect that you or others in your family have been exposed to lead or have health problems such as abdominal pains, loss of appetite, or chronic tiredness that cannot be linked with a specific illness, be sure to request a blood test to measure lead levels. Many health departments in major cities sponsor programs that include lead-level blood tests. If such testing is not available in your community, get in touch with your county or state health department or your doctor for further information.

⁊

CAN YOU DRINK THE WATER?

WATER EXPERTS SEE NEED FOR NEW ERA OF CONCERN
CHEMICALS POISON UNSEEN BOUNTY— GROUNDWATER
GROUNDWATER ILLS: MANY DIAGNOSES, FEW REMEDIES

In hundreds of headlines like these, the "environmental horror story of the 80s" has been brought to the attention of the American public. During the 1970s, efforts by private citizen organizations, governments, and business groups helped clean up many of the nation's heavily polluted surface waters—lakes, rivers, and streams. But groundwater, hidden from view, was virtually ignored. Today, an increasing number of consumers are concerned that silent and unseen contaminants may be "swimming" in the water pouring from their faucets.

About 117 million people—nearly half the population—depend on groundwater for drinking supplies, and the water supply for nearly one-third of the nation's largest cities comes from groundwater sources. A vast majority—97 percent—of rural people get their drinking and irrigation water from wells fed by groundwater. Water is a vital resource, essential for life. So there is good reason for many Americans to ask, How safe is our drinking water?

Individuals or families can get an answer by a relatively inexpensive laboratory test of their water supply. But the problem extends far beyond the tap water that pours from a faucet. In fact, it reaches deep into the earth, where a variety of toxic materials have permeated the soil and polluted the water stored far below the surface.

THE HYDROLOGIC CYCLE

How does a reservoir of water build up underground? All water on earth moves in a cycle. As surface water on lakes and streams evaporates, it rises into the atmosphere and becomes part of a cloud, eventually falling as precipitation— rain, snow, dew, and other forms of moisture. Some precipitation nourishes trees and other plants whose leaves, in a process called *evapotranspiration*, give off moisture that once again enters the hydrologic cycle. Other moisture that falls on the earth may run along the surface and back into lakes, rivers, and oceans, or it may seep into the soil.

Layers of soil hold water in pores, or spaces, that also contain air. But some percolates through to the zone of saturation, or a stratum of earth where soil pores are completely filled with water. This zone of saturation, which is somewhat like a sponge, is technically known as *groundwater*, which moves slowly at rates ranging from a few millimeters to several meters per day. The rate of groundwater flow depends on the geologic formations. Water movement is inhibited by fine clay. But water moves easily and rapidly through coarse sand, gravel, some limestones, and other permeable rocks (geologic formations that allow movement of water).

The upper surface of the zone of saturation is called the *water table*. Sometimes the water table in a shallow zone of saturation reaches the ground surface and then flows into rivers and streams. Heavy rains or melting snow can cause a water table to rise rapidly and force rivers and streams

71

THE HYDROLOGIC CYCLE

Water enters the atmosphere by evaporation from the oceans and other water bodies and by transpiration from plants. Some of the water that precipitates over land areas returns to the ocean in rivers, or through the subsoil as groundwater, and some is locked up in icefields for long periods.

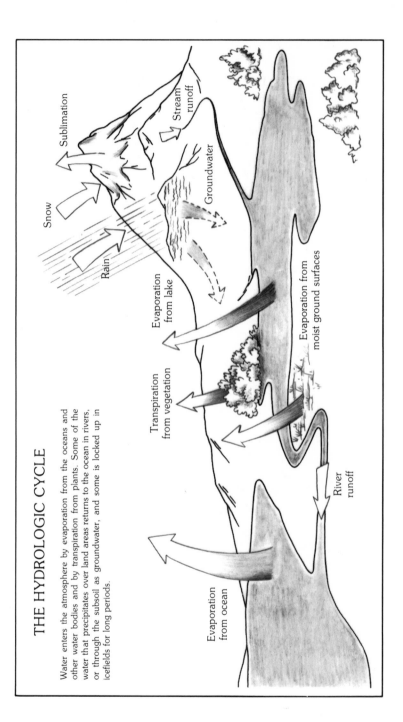

over their banks. On the other hand, a water table may drop if there are dry spells or if wells pump more water from the groundwater source than can be replaced by the natural hydrologic cycle.

When water seeping from unsaturated soil collects in saturated strata of soil and rock it creates a geologic formation known as an *unconfined aquifer* (water carrier). In other words, the aquifer is replenished by water that percolates into it from overlying land. The aquifer is usually undergirded by rocks or clay that cannot be permeated by water.

Another type of aquifer is confined. Geologic formations—such as clays and shales—are barriers to groundwater movement. However, a borehole drilled into the rock can force water up to the surface.

Across the nation these two types of aquifers vary in size and their ability to provide water, and they are steadily and increasingly being tapped. In thirty-five years, from 1950 to 1985, groundwater usage increased nearly threefold from an estimated 34 billion to approximately 100 billion gallons per day.

The largest U.S. aquifer stretches underground from the Panhandle region of Texas north through Nebraska. Called the *Ogallala Aquifer*, it supplies nearly all the water for drinking and irrigation in the high plains region. But the Ogallala is being threatened by "overdrafting," or a withdrawal of water at a faster rate than the aquifer can be recharged. Heavy withdrawals from any aquifer can increase the risk of saltwater intrusion or sudden "sinkholes"—land drops due to declining groundwater that causes soil to compact or settle.

HOW GROUNDWATER IS CONTAMINATED

Until recent years, few people gave much thought to the reservoirs of unseen water below ground. It was commonly

73

believed that the natural filtration system in the earth would prevent pollutants such as sewage from contaminating groundwater. But microbes in the soil, which attack a variety of organic materials, are ineffective against thousands of synthetic chemicals that are potential health threats.

When poisonous materials are dumped or seep into the earth, they mix with precipitation, percolate through the soil to the water table, and then become part of the water supply in the aquifer. Once contaminated, the aquifer can remain that way for decades and may prove impossible to cleanse. Drinking water problems may not be detected until people who have private wells ask for a test or consumers in an area complain of chemical odors in the water or of illnesses that they suspect may be related to waterborne toxins.

Because soils and groundwater flows vary, there is no simple way to monitor an aquifer. The process involves drilling monitor wells, a process which can be very costly, and there is always the possibility that the contaminated water will spread, requiring additional wells.

No one knows exactly how much of the nation's groundwater has been contaminated, but federal agencies say it is about 1 to 2 percent of the total supply. This seems to be a small portion, but according to a 1986 report from the President's Council on Environmental Quality, "it is significant because contamination is often near heavily populated areas where groundwater is being increasingly relied on for a variety of uses."[19]

When an oil spill near Pittsburgh polluted the drinking water, clean water had to be trucked into the area.

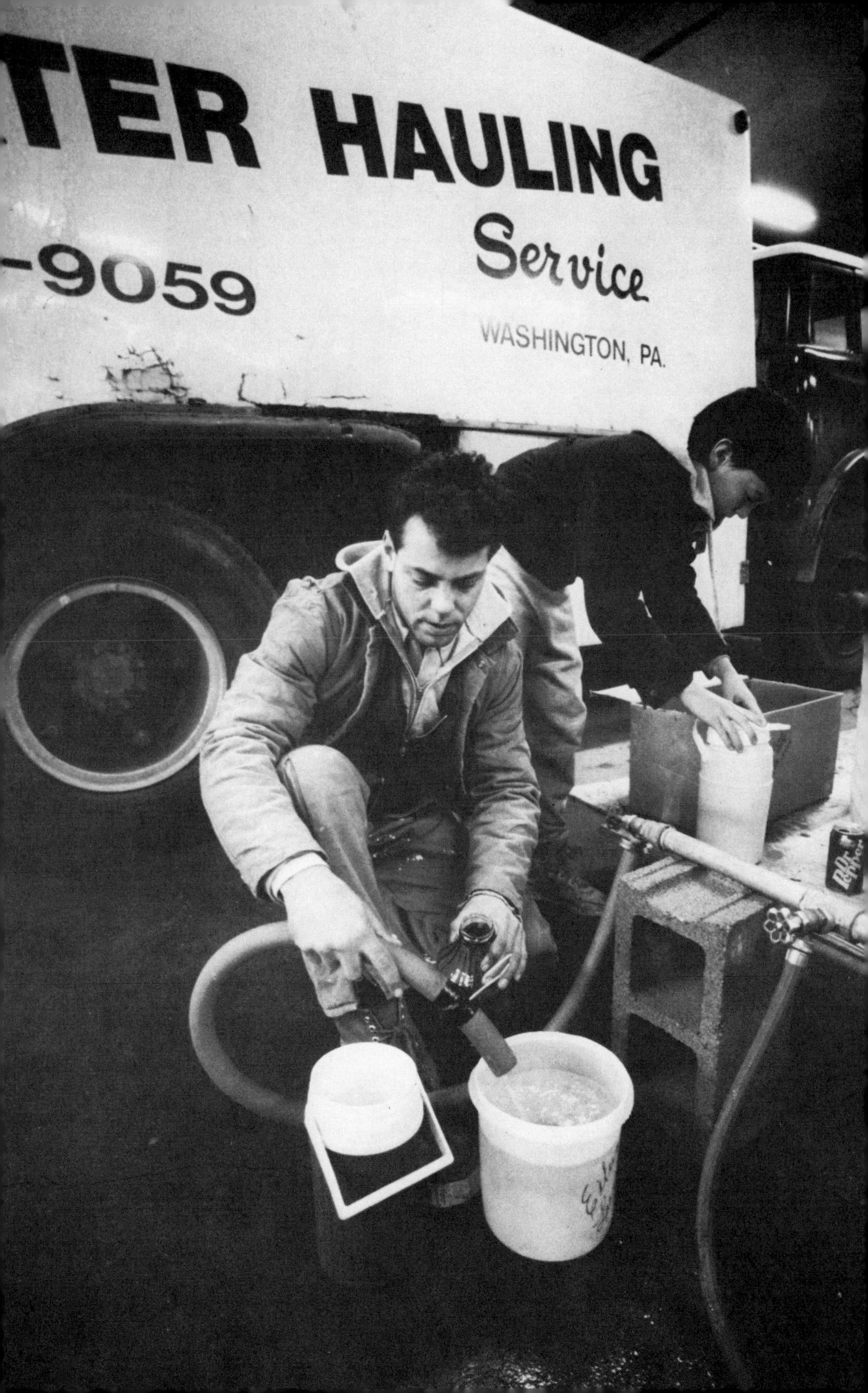
TER HAULING
-9059
Service
WASHINGTON, PA.

*New York City, with a population of over
7 million, is dependent on upstate reservoirs
for its water. Every day about 1.5 billion
gallons of water are piped to the city.*

SOURCES OF POLLUTION

What are some of the pollutants? Where do they come from? The questions are just beginning to be answered. Since 1980 reports on groundwater pollution have been issued by such organizations as the American Chemical Society, American Institute of Professional Geologists, National Academy of Sciences, Natural Resources Defense Council, American Petroleum Institute, and Electric Power Research Institute. Federal agencies, such as the EPA and the Office of Technology Assessment (OTA), which advises congressional members about technical and scientific matters, have conducted a number of groundwater studies and also issued reports on their findings.

None of the research groups claims to know the complete extent of the problem or the number of contaminants or pollution sources. But some reliable data have been compiled. For example, more than one thousand wells in Florida have been shut down because the groundwater is polluted with ethylene dibromide (EDB), a pesticide which was banned in 1983 but is still found in water samples.

New Jersey, New York, Massachusetts, Michigan, Indiana, Minnesota, Arizona, California, and Washington are just a few states that have reported finding high levels of volatile organic chemicals, including trichloroethylene (TCE), in public water supplies. TCE is a component in degreasing solvents commonly used by manufacturers and in many cases is dumped illegally onto the ground or discharged into streams. The TCE then works its way into an aquifer, contaminating the groundwater that feeds city wells and forcing cities to shut down their wells and find other sources of drinking water.

Nationwide there are an estimated sixteen thousand city landfills and seventy-six thousand industrial landfills that are likely to "leak" VOCs—that is, hazardous wastes can leach from the landfills into groundwater supplies. Other major sources of groundwater pollutants across the nation are some 1.2 million underground gasoline storage tanks; the

77

steel tanks can corrode, allowing the contents to seep out and into the aquifers. Abandoned hazardous waste sites, septic tanks, agricultural use of pesticides and fertilizers, de-icing salts used in northern states, and saltwater intrusion into low water tables of coastal areas are additional threats to the purity of groundwater.

EFFECTS OF
GROUNDWATER POLLUTION

Cancer is the most serious health threat posed by many of the contaminants found in well water. Other severe health problems can be traced to polluted water as well. For example, members of a family living near a toxic dump site outside a small New York town suffered chronic headaches and kidney problems that apparently were caused by water contaminated with trichloroethane (TCA).

In other cases, owners of small manufacturing plants in northern Indiana have experienced a variety of ailments, including digestive problems, blurred vision, stiff joints, fevers, and peeling skin, brought on, the manufacturers maintain, by benzene in their water supplies. It is not clear whether the benzene, which is a component of petroleum products, has come from eighty thousand gallons of unleaded gasoline that spilled from a nearby Standard Oil Company terminal in 1979 or whether the source is old oil pockets from oil wells that were active in the area during the 1920s and 1930s.

Hundreds of rural families in midwestern states also have been victims of water contamination. Heavy nitrate concentrations have been found in their well water. The nitrates, which frequently come from fertilizers and are produced in septic tanks, can interfere with oxygen transfer in the bloodstream, putting pregnant women and infants at great risk.

Although contaminated water is known to be a health hazard, it is difficult to establish a *direct* link to specific ailments or diseases. The EPA has set standards for safe levels

78

of certain chemicals in drinking water. But no one is certain what the "safe" level for the *total* number of chemicals in drinking water should be. Nevertheless, it is clear that toxic substances known to be carcinogens and responsible for many other diseases in laboratory animals hardly belong in drinking water.

Once contaminated water is discovered in a community, health department and EPA officials alert consumers and recommend that they use bottled drinking water or install filtering devices in their homes. Or a city may temporarily tap into the public water supply of a nearby community.

Other remedial action may require careful removal of soil contaminated with toxic substances or installation of air stripping towers to remove pollutants from public wells. An air stripper facility forces air through well water so that VOCs break down into harmless substances. Some towers, which may be sixty feet or higher, include carbon air filtration systems to prevent the release of VOCs into the atmosphere.

STRATEGIES TO PROTECT GROUNDWATER

There ought to be a comprehensive law that specifically protects groundwater, say some environmentalists and members of Congress. Federal laws have already been passed to guard against groundwater contamination, say those who insist that no new legislation is needed. Indeed, more than a dozen major federal laws dealing with some aspect of the environment have provisions for groundwater protection. For example, one federal act bans pesticides that can harm the environment. Another regulates the use of toxic substances. Still another controls the transport of hazardous materials. In addition, the Safe Drinking Water Act (SDWA) was enacted in 1974 to ensure the protection of public water supplies. In 1986, Congress passed an amendment to the SDWA that requires states to develop groundwater protection plans.

Nevertheless no single federal agency or state office has primary responsibility for protecting the groundwater that supplies public water systems. But the EPA has set up an Office of Ground-Water Protection to help coordinate efforts of federal, state, and local governments. The initiative for those efforts appears to come from community governments, which are often spurred on by citizen action groups.

Citizen involvement is crucial to any long-term solution to groundwater problems. In communities across the nation, public support for city or county ordinances has helped establish local groundwater protection programs, which vary from location to location. A protection program usually establishes safe storage areas for hazardous substances and mandates that industries and businesses properly dispose of toxic wastes—that is, follow all legal requirements.

A groundwater protection program also requires that farm workers apply fertilizers and pesticides in accordance with label directions and guidelines set by a health department. In northern states, proper application of road salts and deicing materials would be part of a protection program. In addition, long-term strategies include restrictions on the use of underground storage tanks to prevent toxic leaks and notification of local health departments when there are toxic spills. In short, the major concern today is preventing groundwater contamination before it happens.

8
POISONOUS FARM CHEMICALS

While communities carry out strategies and set standards to control groundwater contamination, many also are trying to deal with a related problem: what to do about agricultural chemicals that can be silent hazards to health. Not only do farm chemicals seep into aquifers, they also leave dangerous residues on foods and contaminate field workers and others exposed to toxic sprays.

Worldwide an estimated ten thousand deaths and four hundred thousand injuries each year are attributed to toxic farm compounds, noted a July 1986 *Newsweek* report. Because of long-term exposure to small doses of farm chemicals, millions more may suffer ailments that include birth defects and cancer.

Trying to determine the toxic effects of various types of farm chemicals is no simple matter. People may be exposed to a conglomeration of toxins. For example, you may consume contaminated drinking water and at the same time be exposed to heavy chemical sprays for mosquito or fungicide (parasite) control on gardens or lawns.

In addition, your food may carry dangerous traces of pesticides. To cite one case, during the summer of 1985, California watermelons were contaminated with the pesticide aldicarb, which was illegally applied. Hundreds of people who ate the poisoned watermelons suffered from such ailments as decreased blood pressure, heartbeat irregularities, dehydration, seizures, and loss of consciousness, according to a report published in the *Journal of the American Medical Association.* The entire 1985 crop of California watermelons—$6 million worth—had to be destroyed.

Added to the hazard of exposure to varied farm chemicals is the fact that some toxins can accumulate in body fat. But body fat can store only limited amounts of chemicals, and some may move into muscle tissue or attack the central nervous system.

Yet, the use of farm chemicals is directly tied to the type of agriculture conducted in the United States. The yield from the average farm today will feed seventy-two people compared to seven fed from the produce of the same size farm a few decades ago. Since World War II, the vast increase in the use of pesticides, herbicides (weed killers), fumicides (chemicals that protect stored grains from pests), and chemical fertilizers has helped account for the greater farm yield.

NITRATE POISONING

In most sections of the farm belt, which includes Nebraska, Iowa, Illinois, and Indiana, nitrogen fertilizers are used extensively to improve crop production. But the increased yields may prove to be very costly for some farmers and their families. High concentrations of nitrates from fertilizers have been found in the groundwater of the Midwest, particularly in northeast Iowa, an area that has been carefully studied over the past few years.

The well waters in the Midwest frequently test above the safety levels set by the EPA and have led to nitrate poisoning, or "blue-baby syndrome"—an infant is robbed of oxygen to the brain, a loss which results in death. Studies also have linked nitrate exposure to defects in the nervous systems of babies born to women who have consumed nitrate-contaminated drinking water while pregnant. In addition, some researchers suspect that heavy concentrations of nitrates cause cancer.

USES AND ABUSES
OF HERBICIDES

Herbicides—weed killers—are common agricultural tools in the United States and other parts of the world. A variety of herbicides are used to destroy weeds that absorb nutrients and water needed by crops. Along with weed control, herbicides are a major component of so-called no-till farming. The chemicals are sprayed on the fields so that farmers will not have to plow weeds under the soil to prepare it for planting, thus cutting labor and costs of using machinery, and at the same time reducing soil erosion.

One of the most potent herbicides is paraquat, which is used on millions of acres of cropland in the United States. It has also been used to destroy marijuana fields. Called the "most effective herbicide that exists," paraquat is also the most lethal. Small doses of concentrate paraquat, whether swallowed, inhaled, or absorbed through the skin, can kill. There is no known antidote for the poison if it gets into the bloodstream, although manufacturers of the herbicide claim that a clay mixture is an effective first-aid treatment. Doctors and scientists, however, do not agree.

Manufacturers also insist that paraquat is safe if properly used by certified applicators. The EPA requires that only licensed people apply the product. But the herbicide can be easily misused or incorrectly handled. Sometimes, too, licensed users fail to wear protective clothing when applying the weed killer. When paraquat is used in crop dusting, the poison can drift to nearby areas, sometimes damaging crops, killing cattle, and causing human ailments from headaches to diarrhea.

83

*A railroad right-of-way being sprayed
with an herbicide to kill weeds*

The most widely used herbicides in the United States are alachlor and atrazine, applied mainly by corn and soybean farmers to kill grassy and broadleaf weeds that choke out crops. Low doses of these herbicides cause several types of cancer in laboratory animals, but risks to humans have not been defined yet. Nevertheless, a major concern about the use of weed killers is that they may be a threat to public health: Various types of herbicides have been detected in aquifers and surface waters. Herbicides also may pose long-term health threats to farmers who regularly handle these toxic chemicals.

PESTICIDES IN FOODS

For years common wisdom declared that weed killers and pesticides would break down or evaporate after application and would pose no danger to human health. Microorganisms in the soil do break down some chemicals, and some types of soil will "trap" contaminants. But many toxic chemical compounds do not disappear easily or quickly, especially if high concentrations are applied. A recent EPA report noted that seventeen different pesticides and herbicides have been found in the groundwater of twenty-three states.

Pesticides also show up in the food we eat, even though some highly contaminated produce—such as the aldicarb-laced watermelons—are detected and destroyed. Federal and state laws permit a *tolerance level*, or legal limit, of pesticide residue on fruits and vegetables sold in markets. But during the 1980s the Natural Resources Defense Council (NRDC), the federal government's General Accounting Office (GAO), and the National Academy of Sciences (NAS) released reports on pesticide residue, which aroused public concern over the safety of the nation's food supply.

The GAO audited the methods used by the federal Food and Drug Administration (FDA) to inspect food for "safe" residue levels. According to the GAO report, nearly 3 per-

85

cent of the domestically grown food and more than 6 percent of imported foods selected for FDA testing exceeded the legal tolerance levels of pesticide residues but still reached the marketplace.

In addition, the GAO found that FDA inspectors sampled foods from only a small fraction of the countries that send shipments to the United States. For example, pineapples from the Philippines, a major supplier, had not been tested, even though it is well known that Filipino pineapple growers use a pesticide that is a carcinogen and is banned in this country. Mexico also allows the use of pesticides that are outlawed or severely restricted in the United States, and many Mexican fruits and vegetables enter the United States with illegal pesticide residues.

Yet, no government agency, including the EPA and the FDA, knows how much of any particular pesticide can be tolerated by people who ingest it. In mid-1987, experts were called to testify before congressional committees looking into ways to protect our food supply. Some of the witnesses who represented health, environmental, and citizen groups declared that the GAO and NAS reports show our food supply "is dangerously contaminated." Others who represented food and pesticide industries said the reports indicate our food supply is safe.

SOME VICTIMS OF PESTICIDE POISONING

Every year thousands of farm laborers who handle pesticides or work amid field crops sprayed with pesticides suffer illnesses brought on by chemical poisoning. According to an EPA study summarized in *Science News*,[20] farm workers exposed to poisonous doses of agricultural pesticides known as *organophosphates* experience "depression, irritability and difficulties in thinking, memory and communication."

The EPA study showed that poisoned workers had "difficulties in understanding the speech of others, recognizing printed or written words and remembering the names of objects."

Some farm workers risk death from pesticide poisoning. The authors of *Farmworkers and Pesticide Safety in the United States* described the fate of one victim, a farm worker in Texas. The field hand used a leaky backpack sprayer to apply a pesticide and herbicide called Dinoseb to cotton plants. Because the worker wore no protective clothing (now required by law), he absorbed the poisonous Dinoseb through his skin. Late in the day he fell ill with a high fever. He was taken to a hospital; was given aspirin, which made the chemical more potent; and died within a few hours. Perhaps the field worker's death could have been prevented had medical professionals been alerted to the dangers of using aspirin to treat Dinoseb poisoning. No such precautions were on the pesticide label.

Other victims of pesticide poisoning may be people who suffer from Parkinson's disease, a brain disorder. In mid-1987, scientists began a five-year study to determine whether pesticides and other toxic environmental chemicals do indeed cause Parkinson's disease. The $10 million study is being conducted in twenty-eight hospitals in the United States and Canada and is being funded by the National Institute of Health.

LIVING PESTICIDES

Less than 0.1 percent of more than a billion pounds (about 500 million kilograms) of chemical pesticides applied each year in the United States actually reaches target pests. According to a report published by *BioScience*, the excess "can be widely distributed and may ultimately fall on soil, water, and nontarget organisms." This low rate of effectiveness increases the cost of pest control since broadly applied chemical pesticides also may kill healthy plants as well as beneficial predators and parasites.[21]

When predators are eliminated, some insects and mites multiply. Many are able to build up resistance to poisons and continue to infest and destroy crops. Biologists have developed some food crops that have built-in defenses against insects and diseases. In addition, a strategy called *integrated pest management* (IPM) is also being employed to reduce dependence on chemical pesticides.

The IPM process includes the use of "living pesticides," or natural predators, to combat pests. Using the methods of a hundred-year-old science called *biocontrol*, which has recently been revitalized, researchers try to find natural enemies of common pests. Then they breed the living pesticides on a large scale and apply them to cropland. Scientists also search for weed-eating bugs, microbes that can be put into the soil to feed on harmful microbes, and spores that can kill nematodes, or microscopic worms, that feed on roots of plants.

Work in biocontrol is being conducted at the research center of the U.S. Department of Agriculture (USDA) in Beltsville, Maryland, and in the laboratories of industrial firms already using biotechnology in manufacturing. As an example, a Pennsylvania firm, the Sylvan Spawn Corporation, that develops spawns from which commercial mushrooms grow, is now producing parasite molds. The beneficial parasites destroy molds that make plants shrivel or rot and die.

The USDA also set up two laboratories in Europe, one near Paris and the other near Rome. In the European laboratories, scientists who have come from various parts of the world are conducting research on pests that originated in Europe. The "bad bugs" migrated to the United States with early immigrants who brought their own plants and seeds. The problem is that the insects multiplied, spread, and continue to survive in the United States. But the natural predators and parasites that feed on the pests stayed in Europe.

Scientists in the European laboratories have the task of testing "native bugs" and parasites to determine whether they can be used effectively to control pests such as the onion maggot, asparagus beetle, and alfalfa weevil in the United States. In one experiment, conducted over a two-year period, scientists bred five thousand parasite wasps— "good bugs"—to destroy stinkbugs, which kill tomato plants. In late summer 1987, researchers packed the wasps and sent them to scientists at the University of California at Davis. The California scientists released the "good bugs" into the Sacramento Valley tomato fields that had been ravaged by stinkbugs. There the wasps attacked the "bad bugs" by laying their eggs and feeding on the stinkbug eggs, thus destroying the pests.

USDA officials do not expect "living pesticides" or the technology of biocontrol to solve all of the problems posed by the widespread use and abuse of farm chemicals. Nor do they expect that biocontrol will completely replace chemical pesticides. But there is hope that the increasing use of natural and beneficial parasites and predators will reduce the heavy dependence on chemical pesticides and herbicides. Meanwhile, though, the chemicals themselves must be regulated.

CONTROLLING FARM CHEMICALS

Federal and state laws regulate the use of some agricultural chemicals. However, there has been a long-standing debate over which level of government should be responsible for protecting public health, particularly when it involves pesticide residues on foods. Some health and environmental groups believe state laws should have priority if those laws are more strict than federal regulations. On the other hand, food industry representatives say that there should be uniform standards nationwide for "safe levels" of agricultural chemicals. (Federal standards may be lower in some instances than state standards.)

Another problem in regulating pesticides is determining which chemicals may be manufactured and sold. In 1972, the revised version of the 1947 Federal Insecticide, Fungicide and Rodenticide Act (FIFRA) required that new pesticides pass strict health tests before they could be "registered," or licensed. Any pesticides already on the market had to be reregistered, but those pesticides could stay on the market until EPA tested them. To date, only a few of the estimated six hundred pesticide chemicals now being used have been tested.

Because of growing public concern over what some see as weak pesticide laws, Congress has been under increasing pressure to strengthen the FIFRA. Those who want stricter regulations are calling for a ban on all cancer-causing chemicals used in farming, no matter how small the risk. They also want to prohibit the import of foods with residues of pesticides that are illegal in the United States and to establish programs to protect groundwater from pesticide contamination. In addition, proponents of a tough FIFRA call for better training and more stringent requirements for pesticide applicators as well as protective measures for workers exposed to pesticides in the fields.

9
TOXIC AND RADIOACTIVE WASTES

Dear Friend,
I don't want to alarm you, but our research tells us that a potentially hazardous EPA-listed toxic waste site is located near your home. . . .

So begins a form letter sent to people across the country from the director of the Citizens Against Toxic Waste Foundation, a private organization that is attempting to raise public awareness of the dangers posed by toxic chemicals. Every state in the nation faces some type of health hazard from toxic waste dumps or sources such as industries that use or store hazardous chemicals.

According to EPA estimates, there could be thirty-three thousand dangerous waste sites in the nation. Many are leaking, and perhaps up to one thousand need immediate cleanup to prevent soil and groundwater contamination. For example, in the Kansas City area, a five-acre dump site that has been used over the years for waste disposal by at least three hundred companies now leaches toxic substances into groundwater and the Missouri River.

Another type of toxic site is an underground storage tank for gasoline or chemicals. But few people living in or near an area where such tanks are buried realize there are dangers underfoot—until accidents happen. That was the case in Elkhart, an industrial city on Indiana's northern border. One of the city's manufacturing plants, Accra-Pac, was leveled in 1976 by an explosion and fire. Only the plant's concrete foundation and thirteen underground storage tanks remained. Inside the storage tanks were chemicals, including TCE, used in aerosol containers. Several years later, the same chemicals were found in wells of hundreds of nearby residents.

Toxic wastes also come from multiple sources. In the Great Lakes region, for instance, some 37 million residents tend to have 20 percent higher levels of toxic chemicals in their bodies than people in other parts of the nation. The probable cause? An increasing release of industrial wastes and agricultural chemicals that run off into the Great Lakes, which are used as a source of drinking water.

TOXIC WASTE DUMPS

Love Canal. The name is almost a synonym for toxic waste dumps. Located in the city of Niagara Falls, New York, the canal was abandoned in the 1930s, and through the 1940s became a dumping ground for wastes from a chemical and plastics company. As was common practice at that time, the company covered the chemicals with clay and topsoil, believing they were safely buried. During the 1950s a school and homes were built on the land.

Then about twenty years later, scenes fit for a horror movie began to unfold on the site. The ground collapsed in places, trees and bushes died, fence posts rotted, and toxic muck oozed out of the earth and into basements. By 1978, residents were suffering from a variety of health problems, including skin rashes, birth defects, deafness, and respiratory illnesses.

*A 1980 photograph of a residential section near
Love Canal in Niagara Falls, New York, after families
were evacuated and their homes boarded up*

The New York State Health Department officials investigated and found buried in the canal thousands of tons of chemicals—more than eighty different kinds. One was the infamous dioxin. Toxins were also found in homes. Under federal emergency orders, state officials evacuated people from the Love Canal area and boarded up homes and the school.

The abandoned community has become a tragic symbol for the dangers posed by toxic waste. It has alerted the public to similar health threats. Hazardous wastes are generated by a variety of industries, such as chemical producers, textile dyers, oil refiners, leather-tanning companies, and manufacturers of batteries and semiconductors.

In a recent case, workers at Mattiace Petrochemicals, a chemical plant near Hempstead Harbor, New York, walked out on their jobs because of their company's dumping practices. According to a report in *Mother Jones* magazine, company officials ordered workers to dump hazardous pesticides, paints, and other materials into open ponds that leached poisons into the soil. Workers were also told to empty tanker trucks after deliveries by letting toxic substances leak from tanks, spilling on highways.[22]

In addition to the toxic wastes accumulating from the Mattiace plant, at least seven other hazardous waste sites have been identified near Hempstead Harbor. Mattiace workers and a coalition of residents fear the harbor will become another Love Canal. Cleanup has been stalled by lengthy legal battles that have attempted to fix responsibility for the costs.

WHO PAYS?

Along with legal tangles, environmental and political complexities often delay cleanup and push up costs of toxic wastes. Both federal and state laws control the disposal of toxic materials. The Resource Conservation and Recovery

Act (RCRA), passed in 1976 and amended during the 1980s, sets federal requirements for ways firms must dispose of and treat toxic wastes. In 1980, Congress passed another important federal law that affects hazardous waste disposal: the Comprehensive Environmental Response, Compensation and Liability Act (CERCLA), commonly known as "Superfund." The original legislation set up a $1.6 billion fund to begin cleanup of the nation's worst toxic waste sites. That act was reauthorized in 1986, providing for stricter enforcement and continued federal funding of $8.5 billion.

Both the federal government and industry contribute to Superfund. The EPA determines which industries are responsible for dumping toxic wastes and assesses costs for cleanup, which can vary greatly. It takes about $8 million to clean up the average waste site eligible for Superfund payments.

State and local governments also have agencies—such as regional offices of the EPA, health and environmental management departments, and departments of natural resources—charged with varied duties in regard to protecting the environment and human health. When it comes to toxic waste sites, local, state, and federal agencies may spend years trying to decide which agency should initiate cleanup actions.[23]

For several months during the spring of 1987, *Chicago Sun-Times* reporters investigated the legal and political tangles of toxic waste problems on the city's South Side. According to the reporters, ten hazardous waste sites were identified in 1982 and "are known to be contaminating the land, water and air." Another thirty industrial waste sites may be endangering the area. But, according to newspaper investigators, "Timely responses to the toxic danger get scuttled by disputes among local, state and federal agencies about who is responsible for the waste sites." The agency which takes responsibility for a toxic waste cleanup usually pays the costs of overseeing the project.

Another major difficulty with cleanup of toxic wastes is

pinpointing the source of pollution. On Chicago's South Side, there are so many waste sites that it is unclear who has polluted what. Some waste sites are located on top of older dumps that were used decades ago and covered up with fill dirt. Even if the source or sources of pollution could be identified, it is difficult to hold a polluter legally liable for cleanup costs—unless the toxic waste site is designated for Superfund attention. Then with the stringent regulations passed in 1986, federal and state EPA agencies can require companies that generate toxic waste and are able to afford the costs to pay for cleanup of hazardous materials dumped on their land.

Years of burying toxic materials has created a major hazardous waste site near the U.S. Army's Rocky Mountain Arsenal (RMA) just north of Denver, Colorado. The site has been scheduled for cleanup since 1975. Buried underground in the thirty-square-mile area of the arsenal are such contaminants as pesticides, chemical warfare waste, wheat-killing viruses, nerve gases, and various types of unexploded shells, grenades, and bombs.

How did so many contaminants accumulate in the area? Since 1941, the U.S. Army has used the site for a variety of purposes, including the manufacture of chemical weapons, gases, and explosives for World War II and later the demolition of obsolete war weapons. The army also leased portions of the RMA to private companies manufacturing pesticides. Thus industrial wastes, buried munitions, and accidental spills of toxic materials have contaminated surface

Thousands of storage drums, leaking toxic chemicals, await disposition by the EPA near Louisville, Kentucky, in 1978, in what was dubbed the "Valley of the Drums."

waters and groundwaters and killed wildlife in the area. In 1985, TCE was discovered in drinking water supplied to homes near the army facility.

The army has spent $7 million to decontaminate the public wells polluted with TCE, but this effort is only a relatively small part of a massive cleanup program that will not be completed until the year 2000 at the earliest. In the first place, many studies—perhaps more than one hundred—are needed, army spokespeople say, to put together technical information and to determine how to proceed. (Just an average toxic waste site requires eighteen months to two years of engineering studies before work can begin for cleanup, according to EPA director Lee Thomas.)

For the RMA project, there is also the matter of assigning responsibility. Not only the army, but also the Colorado Department of Health, the EPA, and Shell Chemical, a major pesticide manufacturer which leased land from RMA, are involved in the cleanup operations.

NUCLEAR WASTES

Along with the hazards of toxic chemical wastes are the potential dangers of nuclear wastes. These radioactive wastes emit gamma rays (a form of pure energy), or nuclear particles that can damage human tissues. The amount of radiation, or exposure to radioactivity, determines whether a person will be harmed. High levels of radioactive exposure can destroy body cells and organs and cause death.

Since World War II, mountains of radioactive nuclear wastes have piled up in most states across the nation. The wastes in solid, liquid, and gaseous form are produced primarily by manufacture of nuclear weapons and partly by generation of electric power. Another source is the sandy residue, or tailings, from mining and processing uranium ore used to generate nuclear energy. At least 3 billion cubic feet (about 96 million cubic meters) of uranium tailings have accumulated, releasing low levels of radiation and the decay product radon gas. In Colorado, some of the tailings were once used to make cement and have been employed to fill in land for housing or commercial developments. As a result, radon gas has contaminated many of the buildings.

In the process of generating nuclear power, another type of waste is produced: spent fuel. Bundles of fuel rods, or metal tubes containing uranium pellets from which energy is extracted, are used for only three or four years. Then these spent fuel assemblies, as they are called, are removed from the nuclear reactor. Since the assemblies are highly radioactive, they must be transferred to large pools of water—storage ponds—to allow their radioactivity to decay. At least 1,400 metric tons of spent fuel are generated and stored each year at power plants. By the end of 1990, an estimated 21,000 metric tons will be on hand.

The most dangerous types of high-level radioactive wastes come from reprocessing, or separating leftover uranium and plutonium from the spent fuel assemblies; the residues are reused to manufacture nuclear weapons. Waste products from reprocessing and weapons production are dangerously radioactive, and some particles may take up to two hundred thousand years to decay.

As nuclear wastes have built up over the past four to five decades, there has been growing public concern over where high-level radioactive materials can be stored. Although nuclear power has been produced since the 1950s, no long-term federal plan for permanent nuclear waste disposal existed until 1982. That year, Congress passed the Nuclear Waste Policy Act (NWPA), which included provisions for burying high-level nuclear wastes deep underground.

The NWPA called for two permanent sites in stable geologic formations—areas that would not be subject to earthquakes or volcanic activity and would prevent waste from entering aquifers. A disposal site would have to hold up to 70,000 metric tons of radioactive waste that would be put into canisters, sealed, and dropped into shafts that would be plugged. Later the entire dump site would be sealed off.

DEBATES OVER
NUCLEAR DUMP SITES

Although the law does not specifically state where the nuclear waste sites should be located, congressional lawmakers
had agreed that one would be in the West and the other in
the East. However, after evaluating and comparing "potentially acceptable sites," the Department of Energy (DOE) in
the spring of 1986 recommended three locations—in Texas,
Nevada, and Washington.

Many westerners angrily protested, claiming some federal officials are playing politics and want to keep the waste
dumps out of the East. Many citizens—both East and West—
said they did not want their state to become the nation's
nuclear dumping ground.

Critics in all parts of the nation also have accused the
DOE of performing inadequate and flawed technical studies.
One of the proposed sites in Deaf Smith County, Texas, for
example, runs through the Ogallala Aquifer. Another potential site is Hanford, Washington, a DOE facility that once
produced nuclear weapons. In April 1987, Congress ordered the reactor at the facility shut down because of con-
tinuing safety problems. In addition, radioactive wastes have
been accumulating for years, and many citizen groups claim
that wastes have been contaminating the Columbia River—
a major commercial and recreational waterway. Still other
critics charge that geologic formations in the area are not
stable enough for permanent storage of highly radioactive
wastes.

Yet, there are some communities that would welcome
a nuclear disposal facility. For example, in McDowell
County, West Virginia, where thousands of miners are unemployed, many local officials and residents want the federal
government to build a proposed temporary facility, to hold
highly radioactive spent fuel until a permanent storage site
can be opened. Such a depository, called a *monitored re-
trieval storage facility*, was being considered for Tennessee

100

at a site where a nuclear plant was started but not completed. However, the project was stalled by Tennesseans who feared the temporary facility would become permanent.

The West Virginians, as well as some Tennesseans who support a nuclear waste site, believe the building project would bring up to one thousand new jobs to their area. However, West Virginia opponents, including Senator Jay Rockefeller (D-West Virginia), say that constructing a temporary nuclear disposal site will require skilled workers, most of whom would come from out of the state. Thus only a few unemployed West Virginia miners would get jobs, officials said.

PROTECTION FROM ACCIDENTS AND LEAKS

The problem of where to dispose of highly radioactive nuclear wastes also involves the possibility of accidents en route. If trucks transport nuclear wastes to a single depository, thousands of shipments would be required each year. What are the risks if a truck crashes and releases airborne radioactive material over a community? No major studies have been conducted to find out, although crash tests show that canisters holding radioactive wastes remain intact when rammed into a concrete wall at 80 miles (about 129 kilometers) per hour.

Still, accidental discharge of radioactive materials is always a possibility whether in transit or in nuclear facilities where wastes are produced. Accidents at nuclear power plants have occurred, most notably in 1979 at Pennsylvania's Three Mile Island, where radioactive gas escaped, posing health hazards to thousands of nearby residents.

Many Americans also fear that an accident such as the one involving the Chernobyl power plant in the Soviet Union could happen in the United States. In April 1986, hydrogen explosions at the Chernobyl power plant spewed

101

Following the accident at the Chernobyl nuclear power station near Kiev in the Soviet Union, automobiles are stopped and checked for radiation levels.

radioactive particles that were carried by the wind and rains to towns miles away and across Europe. Thousands had to be evacuated, but not before they were exposed to radioactivity. Of the 458 people studied after the disaster, 31 died. About 90 to 95 percent of the study group received bone marrow transplants and blood transfusions, treatments similar to those used for leukemia, according to Dr. Robert P. Gale, the U.S. doctor who is studying effects of the Chernobyl disaster. Although the treatments have helped people survive high dosages of radiation, Dr. Gale estimates that over the next few decades 25,000 to 75,000 people worldwide will develop cancer and die because of the radioactive fallout from the Chernobyl plant.

Such disasters have prompted many communities in the United States to develop plans to deal with not only nuclear accidents but also toxic spills. For example, in March 1987, a fire broke out at the Spencer Metal Processing plant near Nanticoke, Pennsylvania, 25 miles (40 kilometers) southwest of Scranton. The plant uses acids and alkaloids in metal plating, and smoke from the fire contained sulfuric acid, which can cause skin burns and eye and throat irritations. About eighteen thousand nearby residents were evacuated quickly and safely by an emergency management team. Years before, community officials had set up an evacuation plan and rehearsed it as a precautionary measure—in case there were an accident at the nearby nuclear power plant.

"RIGHT-TO-KNOW" LAWS

Although the Chernobyl accident has added to the urgency of emergency management planning, community disaster planning was prompted primarily by an earlier accident at a Union Carbide chemical plant in Bhopal, India. In 1984, highly toxic ethyl isocyanate, a derivative of cyanide, leaked from a U.S. chemical company's pesticide plant, spreading a lethal gas cloud over Bhopal that killed more than 2,000

people and injured at least 200,000 more. After the disaster, Representative Henry A. Waxman (D-California) called for a survey of hundreds of chemical plants across the United States.

The California congressman discovered that U.S. chemical plants are emitting thousands of tons of poisonous and cancer-causing materials into the air each year. Only six of the more than two hundred different toxins released from U.S. chemical plants are regulated by the EPA, a situation that Waxman called "disgraceful." EPA officials, on the other hand, pointed out that the Waxman survey was not scientific and that the volume of emissions by itself means little if there is no detailed information on the number of people exposed both indoors and out and on what happens to the toxins once in the air.

Nevertheless, many members of Congress and some chemical company executives, along with environmental groups and individual citizens, pressed for federal laws to set specific standards for the emission of hazardous chemicals. The Clean Air Act regulates the amount of lead, carbon monoxide, sulfur dioxide, nitrogen oxides, ozone, and particulates (such as smoke and dust) allowed in outdoor air in the nation's communities. But no law yet covers other toxins.

Some states began in the early 1980s to pass laws giving workers the right to be informed about dangerous chemicals in their places of work. A federal law covering workers across the nation passed in May 1984, and because of the tragedy in Bhopal, India, Congress strengthened its "right-to know"

Blinded by a lethal gas cloud that killed over two thousand people in Bhopal, India, in 1984, these people wait for medical attention.

105

law with the 1986 Emergency Preparedness and Community Right-to-Know Act. The law not only gives the public the right to information about dangerous chemicals in industries, but also requires communities to set up plans to deal with sudden chemical disasters.

A disaster plan includes making an inventory of firms that use or store any of the 405 chemicals that the EPA has classified as dangerous. Nationwide about 1.5 million industries have one or more of the dangerous chemicals. These include many gases used in the manufacture of fertilizers, pesticides, preservatives, medicine, plastics, paint, bleach, and rubber, and in water treatment and food processing.

Most people who live near companies categorized under the "right-to-know" law, are unaware that dangerous chemicals are in the facilities. For example, in a northern Chicago suburb, an official for a high school of thirty-four hundred students said he was not aware that a company just five blocks away stocks a number of highly toxic chemicals. Without a chemical emergency plan, no one could be sure how to evacuate students safely if there should be an accident at the firm, creating toxic fumes or a poisonous cloud engulfing the area. Thus, industries are required to make public a list of the dangerous chemicals they use or store. State officials then have to inform communities about any potential chemical dangers so that local officials can set up chemical disaster plans.

10
CLEANUP AND PREVENTIVE MEASURES

"Every time I turn around I hear about something that might poison me or cause cancer. I just try to forget about it. I figure, you have to die from something. . . ."

Environmental problems often seem so overwhelming that many people would rather ignore them, hoping perhaps that they will disappear. However, environmental problems do not go away by themselves, and, as you have read in previous chapters, efforts are under way to prevent health hazards posed by each of the toxic substances in our environment. On a broad scale, there is a variety of cleanup and preventive steps that can be and are being taken by individual citizens, private organizations, government agencies, industries, and research groups.

DETERMINING RISKS

One of the first and most difficult tasks in trying to deal with environmental hazards is determining what health risks they pose or can pose for the general public. The EPA, OSHA, FDA, and CDC are just a few of the government agencies responsible for analyzing data and assessing risks. In the

107

past, risk assessment frequently meant deciding whether or not a substance would cause cancer or birth defects. Now, however, with hundreds of different chemical compounds labeled as toxic, efforts to determine how a dangerous chemical substance may affect people have become complex.

In the first place, the process of assessing risk may also include economic questions. For example, a chemical plant may be emitting toxic fumes that spew across a town. Should the plant owners be forced to add expensive equipment to restrict emissions? Perhaps the high cost of new equipment would lower profits, leading to worker layoffs or a plant closing. The effects of unemployment may have to be weighed against the health hazards to townspeople.

If, in the case of a chemical plant, the toxic fumes appear to put a large number of people at risk, the solution may be to restrict emissions. But there are other considerations as well. How do toxic fumes (or other potential hazards) move through the environment? How much of a dangerous substance do people absorb or consume?

A computer model can show how a *toxic plume*, or mass of hazardous particles, moves through the air. Analysts also use computer models to determine how contaminants travel through soil to aquifers. But predicting how much of a substance people will consume depends on many factors that cannot be easily measured. In a *Technology Review* article authors Dale Hattis and David Kennedy put it this way:

> *People breathe at different rates depending on their level of activity: workers laboring heavily at a construction site, garment workers sitting at sewing machines, and people sleeping in the surrounding community will all receive different doses of an airborne contaminant. Individuals also have widely different breathing rates and dietary habits, profoundly affecting the doses of specific substances they receive from air and food. Finally, people absorb sub-*

*stances in varying amounts depending on the thick-
ness of their skins and the properties of their nasal
mucous, and even on whether they tend to breathe
through their noses or their mouths.*[24]

Then there is the problem of determining whether a
high incidence of a disease—cancer, for example—exists
among people who have absorbed or consumed a potentially toxic substance. If so, can the researchers conclude
that cancer was caused by the substance? The answer may
not be clear. Perhaps the number of people with cancer is
only slightly above the number who might be expected to
suffer from cancer regardless of exposure to a hazardous
substance. Then researchers may decide the risk or hazard
is insignificant.

TAKING ACTION

Although there are many uncertainties in determining
whether a substance is dangerous to public health, regula-
tors cannot always wait for "positive proof" before taking
action. A case in point is cigarette smoking. When studies
showed that smokers have a much higher incidence of heart
disease and respiratory ailments—chronic bronchitis, em-
physema, and lung cancer—than do nonsmokers, laws were
passed to require tobacco manufacturers to warn users that
smoking is hazardous.

Legal action has been taken as well in regard to other
potentially hazardous products and substances. For example, in late 1986, about one hundred thousand small businesses were required for the first time to send their hazardous
waste to a federally approved disposal site. The newly regulated businesses, which include dry cleaning plants, print-
ers, and auto repair shops, use a variety of chemical solvents.
However, they account for less than 1 percent of the total
hazardous waste in the nation. Owners of small businesses

complain that efforts to dispose safely of such a small amount of hazardous material are hardly worth the added cost.

NEW TECHNOLOGIES

Tougher laws in regard to toxic waste disposal have caused plenty of grumbling in major industries as well as small businesses. Critics of strict environmental laws claim that huge expenses for equipment to prevent pollution have caused industries to fail and unemployment to rise. But there is another side to the story.

In recent years new companies have been set up to capitalize on the business of cleaning up hazardous materials or preventing pollution. For example, companies manufacture emission control equipment set up consulting services to analyze and advise on water and soil contaminants, or develop safe methods to remove pesticides from soils or asbestos from buildings. In addition, some companies have been set up to treat hazardous waste with new technologies. At the Love Canal site, for example, intensely hot gas torches are being used to destroy toxic materials. At a California landfill, bacteria attack hazardous waste. Some toxic cleanup companies established since the early 1980s have developed into multimillion-dollar operations.

Existing companies also are finding that it sometimes makes more economic sense to develop new strategies for waste reduction than it does to produce toxic wastes. According to a report by the Office of Technology Assessment (OTA), reducing waste is quite different from managing waste, or disposing of waste in a legal and safe way. When a company emphasizes waste reduction it attempts to develop manufacturing methods or finished products that eliminate hazardous materials. For example, a 3M plant in Columbia, Missouri, no longer uses toxic chemicals to clean copper sheeting for electronic circuits. Instead the company installed scrubbers—rotating brushes—that clean the sheet-

110

ing mechanically without producing hazardous wastes. As a result, 3M saved not only disposal but also labor costs.

In other examples, OTA pointed out that some companies with printing facilities have switched to water-based inks to eliminate toxic solvents formerly used to clean presses. One firm—Dow Chemical—changed its packaging materials for pesticides from cans to paper. The cans had to be decontaminated before they could be thrown away, but the paper container dissolves in water along with the mixture.

Even though waste reduction can yield economic benefits and eliminate the need to become entangled with increasingly complex laws regarding toxic materials, the vast majority of industries do not seriously consider waste reduction methods. Waste reduction is also a very small part of governmental efforts to protect the environment. According to OTA, "over 99% of federal and state environmental spending is devoted to controlling pollution after waste is generated. Less than 1% is spent to reduce the generation of waste." One reason for the disparity is that manufacturing methods vary widely, so there are no set rules or technical solutions for preventing toxic waste at its source. In addition, for nearly two decades pollution control—managing waste after it has been generated—has been the primary emphasis; there is not broad understanding of how to avoid toxic waste in the first place.

In a comprehensive feature, "Waste Reduction," published in *Environment* magazine, the authors Kirsten Oldenburg and Joel Hirschhorn point out that "State governments have been ahead of the federal government on the issue of waste reduction. In general, they have taken a nonregulatory approach, focusing on educating industry through information and technology transfer and on offering research grants." However, the authors stress that industry has a primary role in preventing hazardous waste and that "it is the people in individual plants and companies who can devise specific ways to reduce the generation of waste."

111

In short, employees directly involved in various operations may have some of the most effective ideas for waste reduction.

CITIZEN ACTION

A University of Illinois professor, Samuel Epstein, who is a leading public-health advocate, agrees that action on the local level is one of the best ways to attack such problems as toxic waste. In a recent speech to Midwest citizen groups concerned about environmental hazards, Epstein noted that he once believed the problems of air and water pollution and hazardous waste could be solved by federal decision making. "All you have to do is draft good legislation, get it passed . . . implement it. Then all the problems will go away. Nothing, in fact, could be further from the truth," he said.

Epstein added that some action is needed on the national level such as the right-to-know laws and government incentives to produce nontoxic chemical substitutes for poisonous substances. However, he was particularly adamant about citizens' using their political strength to bring about changes in industry, especially the vast petrochemical industry. "One of the fundamental strategies of industry [is] preventing regulation of their products," he claimed, adding that another strategy is blaming the victim. "If you get cancer, it's your own fault; you've eaten the wrong foods; you drink too much . . . you're hypersensitive. . . ."

Dr. Epstein was especially critical of manufacturers of the pesticide chlordane. "The scientists and executives in these companies have overwhelming information" on the adverse effects of chlordane—data that show the pesticide is a carcinogen and causes nerve damage and reproductive problems. "Very recently, industry has been forced to admit this, although it had the knowledge on the books for years," Epstein charged.

The way to combat such a "cover-up" is to organize

local consumer, labor, and environmental groups and pressure politicians to take protective or regulatory action, Epstein believes. Apparently his view is shared by many other concerned citizens across the nation since membership in environmental organizations has grown steadily since the early 1980s.

Even though many federal regulations on industry have been relaxed, a number of polls consistently have shown that the public supports measures to protect the environment. In fact, health hazards have become major political issues in many parts of the nation. Citizen groups have formed, for example, to pressure county or state governments to close landfills that are contaminating groundwater. Other groups have tried to educate the public about silent killers in the environment. Some promote political action, urging voters to make their concerns known to officials responsible for health protection—or to vote out of office politicians who favor benefits to industry over protection of public health.

INDIVIDUAL ACTIONS

Some action groups form to publicize the fact that individuals on their own also can do something about hazardous waste disposal. Community groups nationwide have set up collection days so that individuals can safely dispose of their hazardous household wastes, such as leftover household cleaners, pesticides, and paints. After materials have been collected, usually a commercial hauler takes the trash to a regulated waste-disposal site.

Improper household-waste disposal can endanger groundwater supplies. For example, an estimated 200 million gallons of motor oil are drained from vehicles each year, but only about 15 percent is disposed of properly. A large portion of the used motor oil is dumped onto the ground and can end up in waterways.

113

Some household wastes can be recycled. In many communities, recycling centers have been set up to take care of such products as paint thinners, gasoline, used motor oil, and old batteries.

If you want to learn more about the safe disposal of hazardous household wastes, you can order a booklet titled *Hazardous Wastes from Homes* from Enterprise for Education, 1320-A Santa Monica Mall, Suite 202, Santa Monica, California 90401. The cost is $3.75, which includes postage and handling, for each booklet.

To prevent the accumulation of hazardous household wastes, many people are using nontoxic cleaning materials in their homes. For example, lemon juice cuts grease, and vinegar mixed with water makes a good all-purpose cleaner. Baking soda can be used to deodorize carpets—sprinkle it on and vacuum after thirty minutes. Borax mixed with hot water removes mold and is a disinfectant. Scented candles can replace aerosol air fresheners.

You can even "clean" the air with certain types of green plants. Experiments to control pollutants in space vehicles have shown that several types of house plants can absorb a variety of airborne toxins. Spider plants, for example, can cleanse the air of toxic gases such as formaldehyde. The peace lily and Chinese evergreen are other common household plants that can absorb indoor pollutants.

Of course, you can open windows and doors to help cleanse the air in a room or building. But what if windows do not open or buildings are sealed for heating or cooling? An air-cleaning device might filter such pollutants as tobacco-smoke particles and dust. For information on air filters, you can write for a free guide from the Association of Home Appliance Manufacturers, 20 North Wacker Drive, Chicago, Illinois 60606, or consult publications such as *Consumer Reports*. Other excellent suggestions for eliminating air pollutants in the home can be found in a recent paperback, *House Dangerous*, by Ellen J. Greenfield.

Along with books on indoor pollutants, just about every

nationally distributed magazine and countless newspapers across the country have published recent articles on silent killers in the environment and what we can do about them. The consensus is certainly not to bury one's head in the sand, ostrich-fashion. Rather the "bottom-line" message seems to read: Be informed, be alert to potential dangers of hazardous materials, and become involved in programs that attempt to protect public health. To use another well-worn safety message: "The life you save may be your own."

SOURCE NOTES

CHAPTER 1

1. Mike McClintock, "Tight Homes, Bad Air." *Consumers' Research* (January 1986): 27–29; Lowell Ponte, "The Menace of Indoor Pollution." *Reader's Digest* (February 1983): 144–48; and "Indoor Air Pollution." *Consumer Reports* (October 1985): 600–3.
2. John Carey, and others, "Beware 'Sick-Building Syndrome.'" *Newsweek*, 7 January 1985, 58–60.

CHAPTER 2

3. Janet Raloff, "Dioxin: Is Everyone Contaminated?" *Science News*, 13 July 1985, 26.
4. Ibid, 28.
5. Fred H. Tschirley, "Dioxin." *Scientific American* (February 1986): 33.
6. Janet Gardner, "Answers at Last?" *The Nation* 11 April 1987, 460–62.
7. "The Emerging New Issue: More Pollution Indoors Than Outdoors." *Boston Bulletin on Chemicals and Disease*, 1, no. 1 (1985): 4.

8. Jerry Adler and others, "The Dark Side of the Sun." *Newsweek*, 9 June 1986, 60–64.

CHAPTER 3

9. Francine Prose, "Woodstock: A Town Afraid to Drink Water." *New York Times Magazine*, 13 April 1986, 42.
10. "Asbestos in Babies." *Science News*, 9 March 1985, 153.
11. "Asbestos: A Back-to-School Hazard." *U.S. News & World Report*, 14 September 1987, 33.

CHAPTER 4

12. Barbara Farlie, " 'Doctor, What's Wrong With Me?' " *Ladies' Home Journal* (January 1986): 24–26.
13. J. Douglas White, M.D., "Carbon Monoxide Poisoning." *Ear, Nose, & Throat Journal* (March 1983): 7.
14. Charles F. Mactutus and Laurence D. Fechter, "Prenatal Exposure to Carbon Monoxide: Learning and Memory Deficits." *Science*, 27 January 1984, 409–11.

CHAPTER 5

15. Anthony V. Nero, Jr., "The Indoor Radon Story." *Technology Review* (January 1986): 30–31, 36–37.

CHAPTER 6

16. Kathy Dobie and Amy Goodman, "Playing with Poison." *The Progressive* (February 1987): 19–23.
17. Sherry Baker, "Mercury Mouth." *Omni* (November 1985): 24.
18. Charles Schaeffer and others, "Ways to Get the Lead Out." *Changing Times* (March 1987): 14.

CHAPTER 7

19. Marjorie Sun, "Ground Water Ills: Many Diagnoses, Few Remedies." *Science*, 20 June 1986, 1490.

CHAPTER 8

20. "Pesticides May Alter Brain Function," *Science News*, 2 February 1986, 88.
21. David Pimentel and Lois Levitan, "Pesticides: Amounts Applied and Amounts Reaching Pests." *BioScience* (February 1986): 86–91.

CHAPTER 9

22. Steve Chapple, "Take This Job and Dump It." *Mother Jones* (October 1986): 35–39.
23. Karen B. Wiley and Steven L. Rhodes, "The Case of the Rocky Mountain Arsenal." *Environment* (April 1987): 16–33.

CHAPTER 10

24. Dale Hattis and David Kennedy, "Assessing Risks from Health Hazards: An Imperfect Science." *Technology Review* (May/June 1986): 63.

FOR FURTHER READING

(SELECTED BOOKS
AND MAGAZINE ARTICLES)

Adler, Jerry, and others. "Our Befouled Beaches." *Newsweek*, 27 July 1987, 50–51.

———. "The Dark Side of the Sun." *Newsweek*, 9 June 1986, 60–64.

"A Nation Troubled by Toxics." *National Wildlife* (February/March 1987): 33–40.

Alpert, Laurence, M.D. "Is There a Killer in Your Basement?" *Reader's Digest* (August 1985): 115–19.

"Asbestos Debate Goes On." *Technology Review* (November/December 1986): 14–16.

Bailey, Julie. "Is Your House Making You Sick?" *Redbook*, 116.

Baker, Sherry. "Mercury Mouth." *Omni* (November 1985): 24.

Beck, Melinda, and others. "The Toxic Waste Crisis." *Newsweek*, 7 Mar. 1983, 16–24.

———. "A Nuclear Burial Ground." *Newsweek* 16 June 1986, 30–31.

Begley, Sharon, and others. "Silent Spring Revisited?" *Newsweek*, 14 July 1986, 72–73.

Bloom, Gordon F. "The Hidden Liability of Hazardous-Waste Cleanup." *Technology Review* (February/March 1986): 59–66.

Bove, Fred, M.D. "RX for Divers." *Skin Diver* (April 1985) 48.

Brodeur, Paul. *Outrageous Misconduct: The Asbestos Industry on Trial.* New York: Pantheon Books, 1985.

Budiansky, Stephen. "Farmers to Pesticides: Bug Off." *U.S. News & World Report*, 13 Oct. 1986, 69–70.

———. "Uncle Sam's Risky Bomb Plants." *U.S. News & World Report*, 25 May 1987, 75–76.

Burmaster, David E. "Groundwater: Saving the Unseen Resource." *Environment* (January/February 1986): 25–28.

Carey, John. "A Breath of Fresh Air for the Economy." *National Wildlife* (August/September 1986): 37.

Carey, John, and others. "Beware 'Sick-Building Syndrome.'" *Newsweek*, 7 January 1985, 58–60.

Chapple, Steve. "Take This Job and Dump It." *Mother Jones* (October 1986): 35–39.

Clark, Matt, and others. "The Garbage Health Scare." *Newsweek*, 20 July 1987, 56.

Cobb, Hubbard C., and Fiorillo, Cheryl M. "Is Your House a Hazard to Your Health?" *Woman's Day*, 24 Mar. 1987, 30–34.

Cusack, Michael. "No Easy Way to Break Pollution's Chain." *Scholastic Update*, 1 Nov. 1985, 4–6.

Cutter, Susan L. "Airborne Toxic Releases." *Environment* (July/August 1987): 12–31.

"Danger! Radon." *Changing Times* (August 1986): 53.

Davis, Joseph A. "Nuclear Waste: An Issue That Won't Stay Buried." *Congressional Quarterly*, 14 March 1987, 452–56.

Deigh, Robb. "Radon: The Risk and the Remedies." *Insight*, 22 Dec. 1986, 20–21.

Dobie, Kathy, and Goodman, Amy. "Playing with Poison." *The Progressive* (February 1987): 19–23.

Dunlap, Riley E. "Public Opinion on the Environment in the Reagan Era." *Environment* (July/August 1987): 6–11+.

Epstein, Samuel. *Hazardous Waste in America: Our Number One Environmental Problem.* San Francisco: Sierra Club Paperback Library, 1983.

Farlie, Barbara. "Doctor, What's Wrong with Me?" (carbon monoxide poisoning) *Ladies' Home Journal* (January 1986): 24–26.

"For Victims of the Hidden Killer Asbestos, a Manufacturer's Settlement May Prove to Be Too Little, Too Soon." *People Weekly,* 10 March 1986.

Forslund, Janne. "Quality Groundwater for Tomorrow." *World Health* (December 1986): 25–26.

Fox, Jeffrey L. "Agent Orange Study Is Like a Chameleon." *Science,* 16 March 1984, 1156–57.

Fruhling, Larry. "Please Don't Drink the Water." *The Progressive* (October 1986): 31–33.

Gardner, Janet. "Answers at Last?" *Nation,* 11 April 1987, 460–62.

Greenfield, Ellen J. *House Dangerous.* New York: Vantage Books, 1987.

Hattis, Dale, and Kennedy, David. "Assessing Risks from Health Hazards: An Imperfect Science." *Technology Review* (May/June 1986): 60–71.

Hayes, Jack. "Air Cleaners: The Inside Story." *The Saturday Evening Post* (January/February 1987): 30–31.

"How Safe Is Your Home?" *NEA Today* (June 1987): 25.

"How to Rid Your Home of Radon Gas." *Consumers' Research* (October 1986): 26–31.

Huebner, Albert L. "Lead Poisoning—Still a Scourge." *The Nation,* 25 January 1986, 80–81.

Hunter, Beatrice Trum. "Foodborne Illness: A Growing Problem." *Consumers' Research* (February 1987): 11–14.

121

"Indoor Air Pollution." *Consumer Reports* (October 1985): 600–603.

Johnson, Brian. "Tarnished 'White Gold.' " *Macleans*, 9 June 1986, 52.

Kistner, William. "Scrutiny of the Bounty: The Chemical Fog over Mexico's Farmworkers." *Mother Jones* (December 1986): 28.

Lecos, Chris W. "Beware of Imported Foods." *Consumers' Research* (February 1987): 15–17.

Leonard, Burr. "Cleaning Up." *Forbes*, 1 June 1987, 52–53.

Lo Davol, Anna, M.D. "Is Your Office Making You Sick?" *Parents* (October 1986): 230–32.

Loveland, David Gray, and Greer, Diane. *Groundwater: A Citizen's Guide*. Washington, D.C.: League of Women Voters of the United States, 1986.

Mactutus, Charles F., and Fechter, Laurence D. "Prenatal Exposure to Carbon Monoxide: Learning and Memory Deficits." *Science*, 27 January 1984, 409–11.

Manley, Harriot. "Lead in *Your* Drinking Water?" *Good Housekeeping* (March 1987): 199–200.

Marbach, William D., and others. "What to Do with Our Waste." *Newsweek*, 27 July 1987, 51–52.

Matthiessen, Constance. "The Whiff of Waferboard." *The Progressive* (June 1985): 17.

McClintock, Mike. "Tight Homes, Bad Air." *Consumers' Research* (January 1986): 27–29.

Nero, Anthony V., Jr. "The Indoor Radon Story." *Technology Review* (January 1986): 28–39.

"New Teeth in Waste Law." *Nation's Business* (November 1986): 16.

Norman, Colin. "Antagonists Agree on Pesticide Law Reform." *Science* (April 1986): 16–18.

Oldenburg, Kirsten U., and Hirschhorn, Joel S. "Waste Reduction." *Environment* (March 1987): 16.

Palatucci, Michelle (as told to Lisa W. Strick). "My Doctors Wouldn't Believe Me." *Good Housekeeping* (November 1986): 110–17.

"Pesticides May Alter Brain Function." *Science News*, 8 Feb. 1986, 88.

Pimentel, David, and Levitan, Lois. "Pesticides: Amounts Applied and Amounts Reaching Pests." *BioScience* (February 1986): 86–91.

Ponte, Lowell, "The Menace of Indoor Pollution." *Reader's Digest* (February 1983): 144–48.

Prose, Francine. "Woodstock: A Town Afraid to Drink the Water." *New York Times Magazine*, 13 April 1986, 42.

Raloff, Janet. "Dioxin: Is Everyone Contaminated?" *Science News*, 13 July 1985, 26–29.

————. "Signs of How Lead Toxicity Begins." *Science News*, 26 July 1986, 54.

Revkin, Andrew C. "Paraquat: A Potent Weed Killer Is Killing People." *Science Digest* (June 1983): 36.

Rubin, Hal. "Suburbia Under the Spray Gun." *The Nation*, 19 May 1984, 599–602.

Schaeffer, Charles, and others. "Ways to Get the Lead Out." *Changing Times* (March 1987): 14.

Shaeffer, John R., and Stevens, Leonard A. *Future Water*. New York: William Morrow and Company, 1983.

Smay, V. Elaine. "Radon Exclusive." *Popular Science* (November 1985): 76–79.

Stains, Larry. "Stopping the Radon Scare." *The Family Handyman* (February 1986): 20–22.

Stoffel, Jennifer, and Phillips, Stephen. "Double Jeopardy." *The Progressive* (April 1986): 28–31.

Strange, Michael. "How to Get Rid Of Asbestos." *Consumers' Research* (April 1987): 29–32.

Stwertka, Eve, and Stwertka, Albert. *Industrial Pollution: Poisoning Our Planet*. New York: Watts, 1981.

Sun, Marjorie. "Formaldehyde Issue: Back to Square One." *Science*, 1 June 1984, 968–69.

————. "Ground Water Ills: Many Diagnoses, Few Remedies." *Science*, 20 June 1986, 1490–93.

Taylor, Ronald A., and others. "Clean Water: Adding Up the Balance Sheet." *U.S. News & World Report*, 16 February 1987, 22–23.

Tschirley, Fred H. "Dioxin." *Scientific American* (February 1986): 29–35.

U.S. Environmental Protection Agency. *A Citizen's Guide to Radon* and *Radon Reduction Methods*. Washington, D.C.: U.S. EPA, 1986.

U.S. Office of Technology Assessment. *Serious Reduction of Hazardous Waste*. Washington, D.C.: U.S. Government Printing Office, Superintendent of Documents, 1986.

Vietmeyer, Noel. "Plants That Eat Pollution." *National Wildlife* (August/September 1985): 10–11.

Wassertrom, Robert F., and Wiles, Richard. *Field Duty: Farmworkers and Pesticides*. Washington, D.C.: World Resources Institute, 1985.

Weber, Isabelle P., and Wiltshire, Susan D., and League of Women Voters Education Fund. *The Nuclear Waste Primer*. New York: Nick Lyons Books, 1985.

Wellborn, Stanley N. "Pouring Lead from the Tap." *U.S. News & World Report*, 24 November 1986, 70–71.

White, J. Douglas. "Carbon Monoxide Poisoning." *Ear, Nose, & Throat Journal* (March 1983): 6–10.

Wiles, Richard. "Pesticide Risk to Farm Workers." *The Nation*, 5 October 1985, 306–8.

Wiley, Karen B., and Rhodes, Steven L. "The Case of the Rocky Mountain Arsenal." *Environment* (April 1987): 16–33.

Wise, Daniel. "The White Menace." *New York*, 16 June 1986, 52–58.

Ziff, Sam, and Michael F., D.D.S. *The Hazards of silver/ Mercury Dental Fillings*. Orlando, Fla.: Bio-Probe, 1986.

INDEX

125

bestos, 12, 29, 30, 31; and dioxin, 19–20, 22; and farm chemicals, 81–87, 90; and groundwater pollution, 78; and radon gas, 12, 47, 49, 57; and toxic waste, 92, 98, 103

Indiana pollution cases, 13, 92

Indoor pollutants, 15–16, 25, 28, 32–59, 114

Industry: cleanup, 108–113; plant closings, 13–14; toxic substances used in, 13–14, 17–38, 60–64, 67, 77, 78, 91–113

Infant mortality, 31, 32, 82

Insulation materials, hazardous, 11–12, 15, 27–38

Kentucky, toxic waste site in, *96*

Lead poisoning, 11, 12, 60, 65–69; reducing, 68–69

Legionnaires' disease, 15

Legislation, environmental protection, 12–13, 14, 32, 34, 79, 90, 94–95, 99, 103–106, 111, 112

Leukemia, 25, 26, 49, 103

Liver diseases, 19, 22

Love Canal, 92, *93*, 94, 110

Lung cancer, 12, 30, 31, 43, 47, 57, 109

Mercury poisoning, 11, 60–64

Metals, dangerous, 11, 12, 60–69

Methylene chloride, 12, 23–24

Missouri, dioxin contamination in, 17, *18*

Mobile home pollution, 28

National Institute for Occupational Safety and Health (NIOSH), 62

Nerve disorders, 22, 24, 25

New Jersey radon cases, 50, *54*

New York pollution cases, 30, 31, 62, 92, *93*, 94, 110

Nitrate poisoning, 78, 82–83

Nuclear waste, 13, 98–103; accidents, 101–103; dump sites, 99–101

Nuclear Waste Policy Act (NWPA), 99

Occupational health hazards, 24–26, 29, 31, 60–64, 67, 78, 81, 86–87, 94, 105

Occupational Safety and Health Administration (OSHA), 25, 37, 67, 107

Paints, hazardous, 17, 23–24, 25, 65, 67, 111, 114

Paraquat, 83

Pennsylvania pollution cases, 47–49, 50, 101, 103
Pesticides, 16, 22–23, 77, 79, 81–82, 85–90, 97, 98, 103, 106, 112
Pressed-wood products, 27–28
Printing industry, 110–111

Radon gas, 11, 12, 15, 47–59, 99; building leakage, 52–53; and cancer, 12, 47, 49, 57; detection, 52–58; measuring, 48–49; reduction, 58–59; sources, 49–50, *51*, 52, *54*
Ranch Hand study, 22
Reading Prong, 50
Resource Conservation and Recovery Act (RCRA), 94–95
Right-to-know laws, 103–106, 112
Risk assessment, 107–109
RMA cleanup project, 97–98

Safe Drinking Water Act of 1974, 13, 79
Skin cancer, 27
Spent fuel, 99
Stomach cancer, 12, 30
Styrene, 11, 24–25
Styrofoam, 14, 26
Superfund, 95, 97
Sweden, 17, 47

Tanning, dangers of, 27
TCDD. *See* Dioxin
Three Mile Island accident (1979), 101
Toxic and radioactive wastes, 77, 79, 91–107; cleanup, 94–98, 99, 107–115; illnesses related to, 92, 98, 103; Love Canal, 92, *93*, 94, 110; nuclear wastes, 98–103
Toxic Substances Act of 1976, 13
Trichloroethane (TCA), 78
Trichloroethylene (TCE), 11, 12, 77

Unemployment, 108, 110
University of Pittsburgh Radon Project, 53, 55, 56
Uranium, 47–59, 98, 99

Volatile organic compounds (VOCs), 15, 77, 79

Water pollution, 12, 13, 108; asbestos, 30–31; cleanup, 107–115; lead contamination, 67–68; mercury, 61; radon, 49–50. *See also* Groundwater pollution
Water table, 71–73
Watras radon case, 47–49
Waxman survey, 105
West Virginia pollution cases, 20, 100–101